"Written by a nationally recognized expert in the VA system in supporting veteran families, *Coming Back Together* is an empowering, helpful resource for partners of deployed service members and veterans. It teaches cognitive-behavioral skills to help partners cope with a range of issues upon a veteran's homecoming, including intimacy, parenting, communication, and seeking professional assistance. Filled with poignant quotes from family members and practical exercises to spark reflection, this resource is certain to bring practical advice and comfort to many families."

> —**Michelle D. Sherman, PhD**, clinical professor at the University of Oklahoma Health Sciences Center and coauthor of *Finding My Way: A Teen's Guide to Living with a Parent Who Has Experienced Trauma* and *My Story: Blogs by Four Military Teens*

"This book is packed with practical wisdom for resuming your lives together after being apart due to military service. With his deep understanding of the issues families face, Sayers explains specific steps for success in reintegration. You can do this, and he will show you how."

> —**Scott M Stanley, PhD**, research professor at the University of Denver and coauthor of *Fighting for Your Marriage*

"*Coming Back Together* provides expert guidance to couples following deployment. Abundant with clinical wisdom and sensitively written, this new resource helps couples navigate the labyrinth of confusing feelings and unexpected obstacles to restoring laughter and intimacy, and the challenges of creating a new family life that reflects the changes and growth in both partners.

"*[This book]* is a veritable treasure trove of fundamental knowledge essential to restoring or creating a healthy and joyful relationship after the service member returns from deployment. This book promotes understanding and offers step-by-step practical advice that is particularly useful to partners of deployed service members, but that can also be used by both partners collaboratively. It is an essential resource to anyone providing services to military or veteran couples and families."

—**Douglas K. Snyder, PhD**, professor of psychology at Texas A&M University

COMING BACK TOGETHER

A GUIDE to SUCCESSFUL REINTEGRATION AFTER YOUR PARTNER RETURNS FROM MILITARY DEPLOYMENT

Steven L. Sayers, PhD

New Harbinger Publications, Inc.

Publisher's Note

Distributed in Canada by Raincoast Books

Copyright © 2014 by Steven L. Sayers
     New Harbinger Publications, Inc.
     5674 Shattuck Avenue
     Oakland, CA 94609
     www.newharbinger.com

Cover design by Amy Shoup
Acquired by Melissa Valentine
Edited by Gretel Hakanson

Library of Congress Cataloging-in-Publication Data on file

Printed in the United States of America

16 15 14

10 9 8 7 6 5 4 3 2 1   First printing

To the spouses and other intimate partners of those who served in the US military and were deployed far away from their loved ones, their homes, and their country.

Contents

Acknowledgments

There were many positive forces behind the writing of this book.

I want to thank Melissa Valentine at New Harbinger Publications for bringing me the opportunity to write this book, and to Jess Beebe, Nicola Skidmore, Rachel Rogers, and the rest of the staff at New Harbinger for guiding the writing. Their professionalism and enduring positivity were essential in keeping the writing going at what felt like a blistering pace.

My wife, Margaret, and children, Douglas and Kenan, spent many weekends without my presence while I wrote. Their love and support helped me stay focused on the project, while giving me the freedom and space to get it done. Margaret's expertise and input as a child psychologist was essential in the writing of chapter 7 on redeveloping relationships with children. A loving and wonderful experience in my family of origin also provided a solid background from which to understand the challenges that come with transitions.

I want to thank my able staff at Coaching Into Care, the US Department of Veterans Affairs call center, for helping family members and friends concerned about military veterans. Their work with family-member callers has brought to light the concerns and struggles that these family members face. I have drawn liberally from our work in the stories of partners adapted for this book.

The work of many cognitive behavioral theorists and clinicians informed the material in this book and has influenced my career. The seminal ideas and intervention strategies of Aaron Beck, MD, and David D. Burns, MD, informed many of the cognitive strategies I have described. Special thanks go to David D. Burns, MD, author of *Feeling Good: The New Mood Therapy* and many related books. He was the first to show me how important and powerful books written for the lay audience can be. Many relationship researchers and therapists have influenced the methods I have described, including my first professional mentor, Donald H. Baucom, PhD. In addition, Alan S. Bellack, PhD; Andrew Christensen, PhD; Norman Epstein, PhD; Howard Markman, PhD; Scott Stanley, PhD; and Robert L. Weiss, PhD, have all had a significant impact on my thinking and in some way influenced the content of this book.

I owe a debt of gratitude to the military service members who are routinely deployed to far-away places and put their lives at risk in service of our country. I am inspired by their sacrifice.

Foreword

Thirty years ago, when I began my career as a social work intern helping veterans, I encountered a very different system of care than what we have today. At that time, veteran services focused only on the military service member, leaving partners and family members out of the process. At best, partners and families of veterans were tacitly acknowledged by the health care system. At worst, they were viewed as an annoyance to be actively avoided. Sadly, these partners and families were left to solve problems on their own without guidance or help from health care professionals. Thankfully, this has changed.

Today, the family is seen as a critical collaborator in the provision of health care for the veteran. Even in individual therapies for veterans returning from war, inviting the partner or parent of the veteran to join the therapy is becoming more commonplace in many clinical settings. This is significant, since research has shown that veterans want their families involved in treatment (Batten et al. 2009). However, there is more work to do in this arena. Rather than asking whether we *should* include the family in the therapy process, we should instead be asking, *Is there any reason to exclude the family from treatment?* In the vast majority of cases, the answer will be a resounding no.

More than half of our military service members who have served in Iraq or Afghanistan are married. Clearly, the success or failure of these partnered relationships can affect the recovery and successful reintegration of recently deployed military service members. Yet while websites and books addressing the needs of veterans and their families are more common than five years ago and information for military families is more accessible than ever, few websites and even fewer books capture the partner's experience of what it is like on the front lines when his or her military partner returns home from deployment.

Reuniting with a partner after deployment is fraught with challenges. While both members of a couple often experience excitement upon reuniting, they also can experience tremendous anxiety. Psychologists have written about the importance of attachment between a mother and child. And this concept—of a child's need for a safe haven and secure base from which to explore—has been extended to adult relationships. Adult love relationships also need that same level of safety and security. Military service members coming home from a dangerous deployment and their partners who have anxiously awaited their return need to strengthen their relationship bond in order to feel more secure.

After the two are reunited, the questions start to materialize: How have we changed? Does that change serve to strengthen our bond, or will we need to better understand each other in order to thrive as a couple? Can we negotiate our differences and come together to be as strong as we were before the deployment? Can we find meaning from our time apart in order to enhance our partnership?

Steven Sayers, PhD, provides an extremely helpful book for partners of those who have served. Steeped in empirically validated cognitive behavioral principles, Sayers's book beautifully outlines the common challenges couples face upon return from deployment and provides suggestions for how to negotiate those challenges. Incorporating recent state-of-the-art research findings into experiential understanding of the problems encountered by these couples, Sayers provides solutions to issues in an optimistic can-do guide to help couples improve their relationships. The research described in the book is presented in an easy-to-understand way, and it is boiled down to practical recommendations and tips, with an excellent summary of "Final Words" at the end of each chapter. Although the book targets partners of military service members, I suspect that military service members themselves may pick it up and utilize the helpful suggestions provided throughout.

The return from deployment is indeed a difficult transition to make, even in the best of circumstances. It is my belief that this book will provide an opportunity for couples to not only successfully negotiate the challenges of reuniting after deployment but to develop and strengthen their relationship bonds with each other. As a result, their journey ahead will be smoother.

—Keith Armstrong, LCSW
Clinical Professor of Psychiatry, University
of California, San Francisco
Director of Couples and Family Therapy,
San Francisco Department of Veterans
Affairs Medical Center
Co-author of *Courage After Fire: Coping
Strategies for Troops Returning from Iraq
and Afghanistan and Their Families* and
*Courage After Fire for Parents of Service
Members: Strategies for Coping When Your
Son or Daughter Returns From Deployment*

Introduction

I wrote this book for spouses and close partners of military service members and veterans who have undergone lengthy military deployments, either to a war zone or another area that holds risk. You are part of a small and unique group of the US population. Only a small percentage of people in the United States are ever involved in military service, so military and veteran couples have experiences few other couples have. You and your partner have probably experienced multiple separations as part of this duty. Although there are other professions that also involve time away from one's partner, military deployments are different because they hold more risk and offer fewer choices compared to other professions. At the same time, you and your partner may feel part of something larger in the defense of the nation, even though sacrifice often comes with these deployments. As with civilian couples, there is no "typical" military or veteran couple. However, you and other military and veteran couples have many of the same experiences and problems.

The support for spouses and other family members through military programs has increased in recent years, with the focus being preparation for deployment and support during the deployment. If you have already gone through your partner's return from deployment, you may feel that as time goes by, there is less and less support for the challenges that you and your partner face. Most people talk about the reintegration period, or the time in which their partner rejoins the family and community, as lasting a few months to a year after the partner demobilizes. The impact of the deployment, however, can last longer, and you may be continuing to struggle with issues well beyond a year. This book will be useful to partners at any point from just prior to reunion after a deployment to several years afterward.

This book can be used by any type of intimate partner of a military service member or veteran of the military who was deployed as part of his or her service. The book does not assume that the deployment experienced by your partner was to an active combat zone, since most deployments involve increased training, increased job demands, and increased physical risk to the service member. Also, this book will be relevant to partners in traditional or nontraditional close relationships. You may be married, planning to become married, or sharing a household in a committed relationship. Some readers of this book will be active service members or veterans of the military as well as partners of people connected to the military. Still other readers may be part of a same-sex intimate relationship with a service member or veteran. I use the word "partner" to accommodate the wide range of types of close relationships, with only few exceptions in the quoted material presented throughout the book.

This book is based on cognitive behavioral principles as applied to relationships, which means that many of the behavior patterns and habitual ways of thinking that people use in relationships are learned and can be improved through learning something new. The suggestions in this book about communication and making relationships more positive and rewarding are based on methods developed in programs that were thoroughly tested in research with a wide range of couples. In addition, the descriptions of the struggles faced by military and veteran couples are based on years of studies with these couples as well as direct interviews with couples who have gone through the reintegration process one or more times.

The first two chapters are organized by time frame—the period of time anticipating the return of your partner from a deployment (chapter 1) and the first few weeks and months after the return of your partner (chapter 2). If you have already experienced these events, it may be useful to spend more time and effort on later chapters, but there are essential principles introduced in the first two chapters that are built on in the later chapters. Chapters 3 through 9 discuss topics that will be of interest to most partners of those who have been deployed. Your deployed partner may have returned a year ago or more. The problems and solutions discussed in these later chapters will still be helpful for you.

This book is written specifically for the partners of deployed service members and veterans, but the guidelines for communication and other suggestions are also useful for your partner. It is uncommon, however, for both spouses in a stressed relationship to readily agree to work together to improve things, so this book is written primarily to be used solely by you, the partner of the deployed person. Furthermore, you will need to decide if you will let your partner know that you are reading this book and following the suggestions in it to improve the relationship. It is important that your partner not feel as if you are doing something *to* him or her, or changing your relationship without his or her input. To the contrary, most of the suggestions in this book include how you can help the two of you work *together* more successfully, share your thoughts more often, and listen to one another better. Hopefully, your partner will feel that you both have *more* choices about how you want your relationship to move forward after the deployment, rather than *fewer* choices. If you decide to talk to your partner about your efforts, you might make the point that you want to do your best to help support him or her, as well as learn better ways to work together.

You deserve to be recognized for your role as a partner of someone who experienced a military deployment, because you also made sacrifices, even though it was in a less obvious way. In addition, your decision to use this book to improve your own and your partner's adjustment after a deployment shows your continued commitment to your relationship. I wish you the best in applying the suggestions in this book and in accomplishing your goals for yourself and your family.

Chapter 1

The Reunion: Waiting for Your Partner's Return

"You try not to get too excited because you don't really know what will happen those last few weeks—you don't know if *something* is gonna happen 'in-country' or not."

—*Ryan*

"We heard there was some chance that they might not get their 'demob' in time for Thanksgiving, and I was texting constantly with all the other wives in the same unit: 'Did you hear anything? What's the news?'"

—*Claudia*

The time immediately prior to the return from a military deployment can be one of the most difficult periods of waiting while your partner is deployed. This chapter will focus on the issues to think about before your partner demobilizes from a deployment and how to actively prepare for his or her arrival. If you have gone through this already, you will have your own story, but you probably know that it can be one of the most unpredictable and frustrating parts of the wait while your partner is on a military deployment. Many partners of military service members have heard stories of injury that occurred, and worse, after the orders have come to return home. The odds of injury or death are not more likely during this period of time, but it is human nature for family members to think *If he can only be safe a little longer…* or *What if something happens right now?* and have a greater sense of danger for their loved one. You might find that you listen more intently to the rumor mill among other military families in your partner's unit if you are in contact with them, because you are aware that others are also feeling greater anxiety and worry with the news that the unit will be returning.

You know that much of the information about military operations and troop movements is on a need-to-know basis. Even though families can be informed that a unit is returning, exact return times are usually not known or are unreliable. There is often a lot of buzz in the community of families surrounding the deployed soldiers about the return. Spouses want to prepare their children by making sure they are clean and dressed and know what to expect. Family and friends are preparing welcome-home events. Precise planning, however, is difficult during this period. One wife of a returning marine said, "I had already booked a plane ticket and hotel for the place he was going to fly into, so I spent money I didn't even have to change it, just so I would be there when he got off the plane."

Anticipating the Reunion

For most partners of deployed military service members, the service member's safe return is the main focus. But many spouses have some hidden expectations about how the reunion will occur. Naturally, you imagine what the reunion will be like and how you want your partner to react to the children. You may think, *I need to have the perfect outfit; it would be great to just run up and hug him and provide a great surprise with the kids waiting.* You will want time alone with your loved one and want your children to connect right away with your partner. You may be feeling nervous about seeing your service member again. Very close beneath the surface are several worries or concerns, and some of these are based on expectations about how you would like the reunion to occur.

Fears About What Has Changed

You may worry about what has changed between the two of you, such as what intimacy and sex will be like after his return, and how much your partner has changed as a person. If this is not your partner's first military deployment, then you may know that each deployment is different, and it is difficult to predict the impact on your partner. You might also be prepared to feel unappreciated for your efforts in keeping your household together in your partner's absence, and you may feel guilty about this feeling; it is easy for you and everyone to be aware that your partner's sacrifice on a military deployment is seen as greater than yours, so when your sacrifice and efforts are not acknowledged by your partner, it may be hard to say something about it.

One military wife who has gone through several deployments stated, "In the last deployment he was a drill sergeant and came back in drill-sergeant mode, you know, barking orders at everyone, and that doesn't really work at home." Another had girlfriends who had lived through their partners' deployments and said, "I could talk to them and ask, 'Is he going to come home crazy?'" Each voiced the concern that the deployment experience had changed their partner in unknown ways that might cause stress in their families. Talking to friends who have gone through the experience is often a little helpful, but each deployment experience is different and each person is different.

How Your Worries and Concerns May Affect Your Reunion

During the first few hours and days of your reunion with your service member, you may look carefully for clues about "how things will be." Will he be unpredictable or irritable? Will he be distant and cold? Will my partner have post-traumatic stress or depression? Will he start to drink too much? Stories of the troubled combat veteran in the news have become the source of a stereotype, and unfortunately, this produces a sense of stigma, making it difficult to talk about the effects of the combat experience openly. This may create a sense of tension, distance, and discomfort that affects how you talk to your partner when he returns. Your partner may feel scrutinized or questioned because of the concerns in the back of your mind.

Fortunately, research indicates that most combat veterans get through deployment without a mental disorder that requires treatment. Somewhere between 12 and 20 percent of those who had high levels of exposure to combat in recent military conflicts ended up with symptoms of post-traumatic stress disorder, and about the same percentage experienced depression (Hoge, Auchterlonie, and Milliken 2006; Milliken, Auchterlonie, and Hoge 2007). These types of mental health problems are very treatable, and there is plenty of help available. Interestingly, the most common problems actually are associated with the lower back, knees, hips, and other joints, caused by the hard work of combat (Belmont et al. 2010).

Military deployments, in particular ones that involve combat, are life changing to the person experiencing them. There are other books that address how the combat veteran can make sense of these experiences (Armstrong, Best, and Domenici 2006). The more important point now is that both combat and noncombat military deployments mean a separation between you and your service member. Adjusting to the return of your partner from this separation requires some additional thought and preparation so coming back together does not overwhelm you or produce problems in your relationship.

Beginning a New Chapter

Instead of using your observations for predicting what the new status quo will be, you may want to think about it as the beginning of a new chapter. Each time spouses come back together, there is an opportunity to resume familiar, helpful routines—and also to start new and better ones. Yes, there is anxiety that comes along with this, but the more you and your partner see that you don't have to be victims of new realities, the more you are in the driver's seat. Some things you see will indeed be upsetting, particularly at first. You might ask, why is he so quiet? or what is he so angry about? but remember that in transition periods not every new issue or problem is permanent. In coming chapters, I will discuss how to talk to your partner about what you are observing, what your worries are, and what you need from him to remake your relationship over time into a successful and happy union.

You may have to share your partner's time with many other family members and friends. While he has been deployed, you have become aware that you are not the only family member who is waiting for and worrying about the return. Your partner's parents will often be focused on their worry and potential loss, and see you only as a supporting character in that drama, rather than as the soldier's most intimate partner. Their thinking is *This is our child;* you may be thinking to yourself *This is the person I plan to spend the rest of my life with,* and you know that he feels the same about you. Sometimes it is hard to share the planning for the reunion with other family members, consider what their needs are, and still stay true to your vision of what you would like to happen when your soldier returns. It is helpful to consider all the things that may get in the way of the kind of reunion you want in order to prepare yourself for it. One partner of a soldier returning from Afghanistan complained that her partner's mother and sister dominated the reunion, against what she and her partner wanted: "For some reason they thought that showing up with her new baby was going to be some great surprise for him. I could tell from his reaction he didn't really care about the baby—he wanted to see me. Somehow I got blamed for him not caring about it." You may want to have a private initial meeting, but other family members have different ideas about what will make the initial meeting memorable and special. Although homecomings occur in many different ways, most of the time, family and friends want to throw welcoming celebrations, parties, or surprise events for your partner, and these efforts can take on a life of their own without your input. Although to some extent these conversations are out of your control, you may want to do what you can to influence how the homecoming occurs. In this chapter there are suggestions for talking to your family members and friends about the kinds of events and situations that will make the homecoming and reuniting with family members as smooth and comfortable for everyone as possible.

Understanding the Reactions of Your Children

Children of different ages need different things, so you will need to talk to each child with his or her own specific needs in mind. You already know that the children have handled the absence of your spouse differently, in part because of their personalities, but each child's stage in development can determine a great deal about how you approach helping prepare them (and you) for the reunion. Because the place of the actual reunion can vary, from a well-arranged meeting at the home base to an unplanned solo trip by the service member, the situation of the meeting may not be ideal for you or your children.

Infants and toddlers (up to three years old) may not fully recognize your spouse, even if you have provided pictures and video contact with your service member. They might be irritable or cry, primarily because the situation is novel, if the reunion occurs in a place other than your home or one familiar to them. Children this age may not really understand the absence of the deploying parent and may not know the service member upon his or her return. Toddlers may be slow to warm up even if they do recognize their returning parent. Reminders about what will occur, explaining where the reunion is likely to occur, and hand-holding or other physical reassurance may help. Note that children at this age take their cues from the emotions and behavior of the nondeployed parent, so be careful to think about how you express yourself.

Children ages three to six have a greater understanding of the absence of your partner but may have fear or be slow to respond due to the strangeness of the situation during the reunion. They may also feel and act guilty about their parent's absence and may show hesitance about hugging your partner, cling to you, have fears of separation, or have accidents if they are not far out of potty training. Children at this age may need additional hugs and reassurance, and to be told more than once about what is happening. Patience with their behavior is essential since most of the time they are acting out of worry, fear, guilt, or upset over others' emotions that they themselves do not fully understand. Sticking to routines as much as possible often helps, even if that means not seeing their returning parent quite as soon—for example, he may return in the middle of the night, and letting the children continue to sleep is the obvious best choice.

School-aged children who are six to twelve years old have more understanding of why the service member has been away and have a range of responses to their parent's return, depending on their personalities. Some may be hesitant to approach your partner, not appear warm or loving, or cling to you during the homecoming. They may act just the opposite, trying to be the sole focus and talk nonstop to their returning parent or boasting about your partner to others, or they may criticize you to your partner.

Teenagers up to age eighteen might have already been demonstrating challenging behaviors against parental authority, and reunion experiences may be a time of greater irritability or rebellion. They may have several conflicting feelings about the reunion—for example, positive anticipation about their parent's return, but also fear that it may lead to greater conflict or restriction of their behavior. This might result in their being more withdrawn or emotionally cool with their returning parent. Some teenagers might show increased curiosity about your experience as the partner left behind, and you'll need to think about how in-depth you want to go in your responses. You may need to be watchful for high-risk behaviors that teenagers can show around the reunion period and afterward, including problems with the law, increased sexual acting out, and alcohol or drug use.

Coping with the Chaos: Ways to Prepare

What will you be able to do about these situations? Decide the things you can influence and decide to practice acceptance and positive forms of coping for the rest. There are several parts to successful coping, including making the best plans (and backup plans) possible and then making peace with the outcome of events, adjusting to your own attitude, and using your supports and resources.

Concerns About Reunion and How to Cope with Them

Concern: The period of time between getting orders to return from a military deployment to the time of reunion feels more dangerous than the rest of the deployment.

Coping response: Remind yourself out loud that there is no logical reason this time period is more dangerous than the rest of the deployment. Avoid "what if" questions that get you worried during this period of time.

Concern: The details of the return of your service member from deployment can be unclear or unknown.

Coping response: Resolve that the way your partner's return occurs will not be fully known and that you will find positive ways to prepare yourself and your family while you wait.

Concern: Many people may want and demand your partner's time and attention.

Coping response: Think about what your and your children's needs are for time with your spouse or partner; then talk with your partner's parents and siblings and let them know what you are thinking. Decide how much you want to be involved in the events and conduct your planning accordingly.

Concern: Because of the unpredictability of the return from deployment, seeing your partner again may not go as you planned.

Coping response: Allow for many different scenarios and be flexible. Make backup plans and have frequent discussions with your partner about what kinds of social events he prefers in the first hours and days of the reunion.

Concern: Children of different ages need different types of discussions about what to expect and how to help ease the return.

Coping response: Have several discussions with your children about what will occur and listen carefully for their concerns and feelings.

Concern: There may be several unexpected events associated with the reunion with your partner, as well as upsetting actions on the part of family members and friends.

Coping response: Use your emotional supports, including those associated with your partner's unit and service-related resources, as well as resources outside your military network.

Talking to Family Members

The homecoming events that occur are first among the things you may be able to influence for your service member when he arrives home. In addition to a homecoming event that may be planned for the whole unit, other family members may want to put together additional parties and celebrations for your partner's return. This may leave you with very little private time. Fortunately, although your partner may appreciate some parties and homecoming celebrations, his preference will likely be to keep these limited. You may not be able to communicate well with your partner near the end of the deployment, and he may not want to talk much about the topic because the focus during his service has been on his work. But any increased information about what he wants upon returning will help you communicate this to your family and friends. Second, gaining some understanding of your partner's experience will help you communicate your preferences clearly to friends and family prior to the return. Many service members returning from deployment, especially those returning from combat deployments, have complicated and conflicted feelings about their service (Armstrong, Best, and Domenici 2006). Too many celebrations may lead them to feel uncomfortable or undeserving. Often they may feel that it is not possible for others to understand their deployment experiences and therefore do not want to face a lot of questions about their combat actions. The return to civilian situations is often sudden and jarring. Others may be filled with relief and a desire to lay low for a while. Describing to family members and friends ahead of time what your partner will likely be experiencing will help you smooth the conversation about the first greeting and welcoming events that follow. To the extent that you can, communicate these wishes to your partner's friends and family members, and then you may be able to influence what happens. Ask your friends and your partner's family members to consider how much your spouse may simply want to rest. Being around too many people for too long at too many events may quickly become tiresome. If you have been able to communicate with your partner as the end of the deployment nears and hear his concerns about reunion events, convey these wishes to the extended family.

Making Plans (and Backup Plans)

Despite the potential for unpredictability of your initial reunion with your partner, it is a good idea to make plans to celebrate with him or her in a more intimate way. You might want to arrange something special to celebrate the return—a special meal, homecoming gift, or activity. If you have children, involving them in these plans will help the family make the time around homecoming special. If you've planned to make a special meal for your partner, you might wait until he is home and rested before suggesting you serve this meal or make sure it can be delayed until the best possible time.

Plan to continue to talk to your partner and your family members about building in flexibility for events, especially after your partner is at home. Avoid packing the schedule too tightly, as your partner likely will be looking for a relief from the demands of a difficult deployment schedule and the rigors of travel home from a distant time zone. Let him know that when ready, you would like to talk about what plans have developed and to find out what events will be comfortable. This might be a frequent discussion. Alert family members that plans may need to change based on the energy level of your service member after the return home.

In addition, despite your best efforts to make special plans, to present the children in their best outfits, and to influence the type of homecoming your partner has, do not be surprised if he does not at first notice your efforts. Your partner is likely to be tired, having traveled under difficult circumstances across several time zones. Recognition of the work you put into influencing the homecoming events or situations will most likely come at a later time, especially as he learns about the situation surrounding the preparations for his return and all the work that went into it. It is also possible that the more successful you are in making the homecoming smooth, the less your efforts will be visible. The best reward may come in knowing that you did your best in preparing for a positive homecoming for your partner.

Talking with Your Children and Preparing for the Reunion

As I discussed above, children of different ages need different things. For all, remember that multiple conversations are usually best. Be prepared to give your children plenty of opportunity to comment, ask questions, and express concerns and worries. Below are some basic ideas about handling the reunion with your partner and your children.

With younger children up to age six, it is important to recognize that you may have to wait for the reunion with your partner in a place less familiar to the children, such as an airport or some venue with other families of service members. Listen to your children's objections or signals of distress, such as whining and complaining, and be accepting of the fact that they are uncomfortable, worried, or afraid, and not acting up or being bad. Treat these types of behaviors as a prompt for you to be interested, curious, and caring about what your children are experiencing, rather than as behaviors needing punishment. Ask lightly, "Can you tell me what's the matter? What's upsetting you?" Reassure them about the amount of additional time needed in that situation, or help distract them with a game or activity.

Expect that during the reunion, they may need some time to warm up to their returning parent. Because the youngest kids in this age range may not recognize their returning parent, think of it more as a reintroduction than a reunion. This might mean holding younger ones as you hug your partner. Avoid forcing older children in this age range to hug your partner; instead help your service member to find a way to greet your children at their level, such as sitting or kneeling.

Children ages six to twelve will need greater discussion of what to expect and how to best interact with their parent. If he or she is excited and overtalkative, your school-age child might need guidance on when to step back and let others interact with your partner. If he or she is hesitant or cautious, give the message that it is fine to take some time in approaching the returning parent. You can give encouragement and reassurance that your service member partner wants to know about the child's activities in the past months when things have settled down. You can help the conversation by suggesting to your partner that he ask your school-age child about a particular recent event at school or after-school activity. Other children will want to rush up and hug their returning parent—most military family readiness programs coach family members to remind kids not to run up to their returning soldier or rush them from behind. As one mother stated, "I reminded my kids not to rush up to their father from behind because he may be surprised and have a quick reaction that he does not mean."

As discussed above, teenagers may have conflicting feelings about the reunion and may show more challenging or rebellious behavior during this period. You might be especially careful to listen for comments about their concerns without being immediately critical or questioning. You can still make clear what your expectations are (for example, attendance at reunion events, being respectful) but take care not to be overly restrictive or punishing for minor infractions or moody behavior.

Some of your conversations with your children may result from purposely sitting down with them to talk about your partner's return to let them know how it may work, where they are likely to see their absent parent again, and so on. Often, such conversations occur when you least expect them—while driving your children in the car, as you are preparing dinner, and when saying goodnight. Be ready to listen, and be careful not to interrupt or correct your child if you hear a worry that is upsetting to you. For example, your child might ask, "Will Dad be different when he gets home?" or "Will Dad remember me?" or "Did Mom get hurt?" Make sure you follow up any questions that are not clear so you really understand what the concern is: "It sounds like you are worried about Dad (or Mom). Can you tell me what your worry is?"

You will naturally want to provide reassurance, but you also know there are many unknowns, and you have worries of your own. It is often enough to reassure kids about their most basic fears while at the same time acknowledging that parents cannot promise that nothing will change or that there will not be any challenges. There are several ways this might be said, including, "I know you are worried about how it will be when your father gets back. There are lots of good things about being a family again, but there are some things that may feel different or new. We'll work really hard to make sure that things go as well as possible. I do know that your dad loves you and misses you even though he's had to be away for a long time."

Coping: Attitude Adjustment and Using Your Resources

Coping with stress involves reducing the intensity and frequency in which you are upset about events. There are several ways to cope with the stress of anticipating and planning for the reunion with your partner. The discussion above focused on trying to change the situation so upsetting events occur less often—for example, your extended family might intrude less on the reunion events because you explained to them what your partner will need during that period. Other ways of coping focus on changing your response to unpleasant events so that you are less upset and upset for a shorter period of time. This does not mean, of course, that these events will no longer be important to you but just that they will not continue to plague you weeks, months, and years after they occur.

Attitude Adjustment

First, it is important to recognize that reunions are themselves temporary events. Because the reunion occurs in a brief space of time, nothing that occurs in that time frame should be seen as permanent. Upsetting events are not necessarily a sign, a trend, or an enduring situation. For example, you might be surprised that your returning partner is upset about the behavior of the children or may seem less excited or thrilled to see you than you expected. Your disappointment in this can turn to fear and anger if you believe it is an indication about how your partner will be from that point onward. An alternative view, however, is that there may be many things that determine how your partner reacts during the first reunion with you and the children, from the length of the flight home to thoughts about a tough deployment or many other factors. Single reactions can sometimes be projected into the future around such important events like a reunion after a long absence.

Second, as discussed above, a useful attitude is that a reunion is a beginning of a new chapter for you and your partner. It is an opportunity for resuming good habits and changing less useful ones. Furthermore, seeing yourself and your partner as key actors in the development of this new chapter in your relationship is part of this attitude. Most people do not consider that relationships change, usually because we all have habits and attitudes that are enduring. But because of important events and changing circumstances, relationships always change over time. Seeing yourself as a decision maker in how your relationship changes puts you at a great advantage when negative events occur. For example, if you and your partner have an immediate disagreement about the children soon after reuniting, you can know that there is plenty of time for developing new ways of working better together as parents.

Using Your Resources

Seeking the support of others who understand and can help you before and during your reunion with your service member is also an excellent way to cope. The secret here is to identify what kind of support you need and who can provide it. There are at least two types of support: practical help with tasks you need to do; and emotional support, in which people who know what you are going through are able to listen to you talk about your concerns and sympathize.

During preparations for the reunion from a military deployment, the partner who remains behind may be reluctant to ask for help, in part because of the overall success experienced in managing the household during deployment. This is the idea that one can "handle it all." Ironically, it may be the best time to ask for help from extended family because of the motivation everyone in the family has about preparing for the return of a service member. Examples of practical help might include watching children, transportation to the site where the reunion is to occur, preparing the house, and assistance with relocating out of temporary housing to the place in which you and your partner will now live.

One decision you will have to make as you consider who can provide emotional support to you is whether it is best to confide in those who are part of your military support network or others outside this network. If you have the luxury of having friends you can talk to outside the military social structure, you have the advantage of being able to complain about the support system for families without worrying that your complaints will travel beyond that private discussion. An advantage of talking about your worries with another spouse of a service member is that your friend may be experiencing very similar issues. If you have the benefit of both sources of support, consider carefully choosing with whom you share which type of worries.

Finally, you are likely aware that the command structures of most military units and bases ensure various types of supports for family members, depending on the military branch and whether your service member is typically part of the active duty military, National Guard, or reserves. There are various additional educational and other types of supports available for families listed in chapter 9.

Final Words

There are a range of ways of improving your reunion experience with your service member, but the most important factor includes your realization that it is a small part of a new phase in your relationship rather than an end in itself. You are encouraged to review the section "Concerns and How to Cope with Them." The points made in this chapter address actions you can take to lower your stress level about the reunion and to move through it with the fewest bruises possible. Starting in the next chapter I will discuss in more depth the ways in which you can work with your partner to rebuild your relationship.

Chapter 2

When Your Partner First Returns

"After he got back, we had to move to another base for a couple of months. Then we had to move again, so it was hard to establish a new base of support and feel settled."

—*Rochelle*

"He came home thinking it should be perfect, like every holiday was supposed be the way he envisioned; I had a tough time making him realize things aren't always going to go as planned."

—*Katy*

O nce your partner is safely at home, there is often a great deal of relief and happiness that can move your family forward to the next phase in your lives. There will also be challenges and the need to understand and deal with these challenges. There are several things to know about the first period of adjustment after the return. This chapter will focus on factors that may determine how well your adjustment goes during the initial phase of your service member's return to the household.

Common Effects in the Initial Period of Reintegration

Each couple that experiences reintegration after a military deployment has a unique set of circumstances, yet there are some common experiences as well. Below I discuss some issues to consider during the first several months of your partner's reintroduction into your household.

Different Pathways During the Initial Period of Reintegration

There are several ways couples can experience the initial period after a military deployment. The different pathways appear to follow a small number of patterns (MacDermid 2006). Recent research suggests that fewer than half of families experience a "honeymoon"—an initial highly positive feeling followed by a lower period of functioning and a recovery period. Those who did, however, report that the low points during the first year occurred between four and nine months after the return. Others experienced a consistently high level of adjustment that continued in an even fashion across time. Still others had up-and-down experiences during the first year after the deployment. Another important point to remember is that your partner may have a different view than you of how your reunion and the reintegration of your family is going. Even though you may be feeling frustrations, your partner may be still feeling the relief of returning from the deployment.

Each person's situation is different. Most families have challenges, and some variation in how things go between you and your service member over the weeks and months after your reunion is the most likely scenario. Also, expect that most families end up recovering well after dealing with their challenges and that some will have challenges requiring professional help. How well you feel things are going at any given moment in the first year is not the most reliable way to determine whether to get professional help or how things will be at the end of the first year after your reunion. For now, let us explore the factors that may determine how well things go after your reunion with your service member.

Preexisting Issues Can Make You Vulnerable

The vast majority of studies of returning combat veterans and their family members show that those with existing difficulties prior to the deployment were more likely to face these or other difficulties after the return of the service member. One wife of an army corpsman described her service member husband as "dealing with depression since before we met" anticipating that this would continue to be something the couple needed to monitor and manage. Any military deployment, especially a combat deployment, is likely to involve greater stresses than time at home. After leaving deployment, your partner my feel less supported without the intense interaction with her unit. The risk that your partner will experience the kind of difficulty she had prior to deployment is naturally higher. Knowing how these issues may have an impact on you and your partner can help you focus on areas that may need your attention as a couple, and perhaps on getting support from professionals.

There are several common findings in the research about the kinds of preexisting problems and their impact on adjustment after the deployment. Couples that should anticipate the most problems after deployment are those who married young, have less educational preparation, and have a history of marital problems prior to deployment (Karney and Crown 2007). Having several previous combat deployments is also a risk factor. These all have a negative impact because each of these issues may leave your relationship less prepared to weather problems that may come up after your reunion. If you already find it tough to resolve problems in your relationship, things will become more difficult as time goes on, unless you learn more effective problem-solving and communication strategies.

There are other factors after deployment that can also make the adjustment harder for you, including situations that lead to less support for you or your partner (for example, multiple moves). If you or your partner have injuries or disabilities that lead to financial stress, then your initial adjustment period may suffer. But what do you do about these factors? Be aware that they each have an impact, and use the suggestions in this book to strengthen your and your partner's ability to cope, adjust, and work together better as a team.

If any physical conflict occurred between you and your partner before the deployment, this type of conflict might increase afterward. Any physical conflict between you and your partner is considered not part of a healthy relationship, even pushing and throwing things in anger. Although many people would consider pushing and throwing things to be minor problems, they still may lead to someone getting hurt, even when this is not your or your partner's intention. It is also important to know that feeling threatened or forced, even threats not involving physical force, is a corrosive pattern for your relationship. The good news is that in most cases, you and your partner can work together to limit this type of conflict, and it does not necessarily mean you and your partner must separate in order to be free of it.

The Expectations and Other Perceptions in Determining Adjustment

The ways in which we view and understand the world determine a great deal about how we feel. Often we take our views without questioning them, but when we do, we risk feeling worse about things than is necessary. Knowing this gives you an opportunity to reexamine and consider better ways of viewing the return of your partner.

Expectations

Many of your feelings and reactions during this time of adjustment may depend on your expectations and when problems do crop up, on your beliefs about why you and your partner are having difficulty. Perhaps because of the initial euphoria of homecoming, there is the lore of a honeymoon period in which everything is great, easy, and pleasurable. Although having your partner back is much better than her being deployed, you are likely too savvy to be unaware that some problems might occur. The way you receive or view problems that occur may have an impact on your unhappiness and your ability to manage problems when they arise.

What are your expectations about how things will go with you and your partner? Think about whether you anticipate having difficulty in the weeks and months after your reunion with your partner or whether you believe your relationship will pick up where it left off. What source of information has led to your belief about how things will be? Other military spouses? Your reading about deployment experiences of families? Discussions with military family life educators? Your past experiences of your partner deploying? What expectations do you have of your partner: To allow you to continue running the house in the same way as you have been running it? To relieve the burden you have had in running the house in her absence? Later chapters will guide you through the process of working out with your partner how things will proceed.

Interpretations

A concern of some spouses is how to interpret their partner's quietness and lack of openness about feelings and recent deployment experiences. How open and revealing your partner may be in letting you know what she is upset about is determined by many factors, including individual differences, the impact of combat experiences, and having been away from the family on deployment. Recent research by Keith Renshaw and Sarah Campbell at George Mason University suggests that it is commonly upsetting when partners *withdraw* from interaction with their spouses and families, and when they appear to be experiencing *no emotion* (Renshaw and Campbell 2011). How you interpret this is key. If you interpret this as being caused by you or your relationship and as an indication of an unsolvable problem, then you are much more likely to be upset by it, and have difficulty responding well to changes in your partner and challenges in your relationship. Another factor in this research is whether you are aware of how difficult the deployment was for your partner. Partners in this research study who believed that a combat deployment involved many difficult and traumatic situations were less distressed with the relationship and their partner after reunion and able to be much more sympathetic than those who felt the deployment involved very little combat or stressful situations (Renshaw, Rodrigues, and Jones 2008). What does this mean for you? If you are upset with your partner because of disagreements after your reunion or because of how your partner is treating you, take a step back. Unless you are fully aware of all the situations your partner faced while on deployment, you may not have all the information you need—I will present several reasons she might have not talked about everything that happened. You might feel less angry and better able to work with your partner as a team to resolve a disagreement.

Alternative Explanations

What are the alternative ways of understanding this type of behavior? First, don't make the assumption that your partner knows what she is feeling all the time and is simply keeping it from you. Second, her silence may have more to do with transitioning from deployment and being careful about revealing important and traumatic details. One spouse reported: "I only heard about a few of the bad firefights, and I think I got the sanitized version; I overheard him talking to his buddies, and those firefights were much worse than I thought." Recent research I and my colleagues have conducted with combat veterans indicates that your partner also understands that when she is less communicative because of feelings of depression or even a lack of feelings of emotion, it may lead to more problems in adjusting to the family (Sayers et al. 2009).

Family Reintegration Is an Ongoing Activity

As I have hinted, your partner may have minor or even major reactions to the trauma of combat experienced on deployment. This is important for several reasons. First, you care about your partner and feel the burden of her pain. This reason is clear and easy to understand. Second, your partner may act in ways that are uncharacteristic around you and your children, such as being more irritable or wanting to be less involved at home both emotionally and physically. These are upsetting behaviors, and you may end up feeling annoyed or hurt. Third, and most important, reactions to trauma can often lead to your partner being less able and willing to work with you as a team to adjust to the new situation. This is wrapped up in the idea of reintegration as an activity—a set of things one can actually do, as opposed to a period of time in which you wait for things to become normal again. Below, I discuss this idea of reintegration and how trauma reactions might get in the way.

Reintegration after your partner returns from a military deployment is not a passive process; that is, you and your partner are not just waiting to get used to one another again. It may seem like this because certainly part of the time in the first several weeks and months you are practicing patience, watching, and waiting to see how things will go. The active part of the process, however, is when you form an opinion or belief, make a decision to act, and talk with your partner about how things are and how you want them to be. In short, you are trying to make adjustments to make sure your relationship and family are as happy and successful as you can make them.

It is helpful to describe all the areas in which you and your partner are restarting old routines and charting new ones. First, you and your partner are learning to be intimate again, both emotionally and physically. Neither of you has been able to be as intimate during deployment, and many service members stop sharing many of their thoughts and feelings even prior to deployment as they increase their training time and steel themselves emotionally for combat. Opening up again is difficult for each of you because it involves being vulnerable, and as we will discuss, your partner may be less open with personal information as a matter of training and combat preparation. Second, routines within the family (for example, dinnertime, bedtime, movie night, when chores are done) changed when your partner left. They will likely change when your partner returns. Will you and your partner negotiate how this new routine works, or *if* it works? Third, the distribution of duties such as bills, cooking, and taking care of the house certainly changed when your partner was deployed and may be leading to some pride on your part for handling the responsibilities as you did. Fourth, you likely made the day-to-day and major family decisions when your partner was away, and your partner probably wants her influence back either quickly or perhaps after some time. How will you and your partner decide who will make sure your children do their homework, what their summer activities will be, and how to respond to their negative behavior?

Each of these situations requires some response from you, the decision either to step back, to assert yourself, or to negotiate with your partner. This assumes, however, that your partner is willing to talk with you when you want to negotiate, to share influence, and to let you know how she feels about a situation. This becomes more complicated if your partner's attention is on her own challenges, such as feelings and reactions associated with traumatic combat events or the chronic physical pains associated with injuries from battle. Furthermore, withholding feelings and withdrawing from discussions or from day-to-day interaction may be direct outcomes of reactions to trauma. These reactions would likely make you and your partner's reintegration efforts more of a challenge. Fortunately, you can take an active role in addressing this problem. But first you will need to lay the groundwork before deciding that this is the problem.

What You Can Do to Begin Adjusting

The suggestions below are the beginnings of skills that you will learn as part of this book, and they are very easy to implement. Be aware, however, that simply thinking about what you are reading will not give you as much benefit as actually doing these activities. The more you commit pen to paper and experiment with a suggested way of talking with your partner, the more you will benefit and change in a desired direction.

Clarify Your Worst Fears and Identify Your Expectations

Set aside just a few minutes to clarify in your own mind what your worst fears are about how things will develop with your partner. Sit down with pen and paper and write these thoughts in a list without editing them. Are you worried that you and your partner will get divorced? That your partner's military training will have a negative effect on the patterns you developed with the kids when she was away? Are you worried that your partner will have a tough time getting employed? It is important that you not inhibit your thoughts. You can keep the paper private or even simply destroy it after you have written your worries down. The idea is to be honest with yourself so you know what fears are making it hard for you to consider your options calmly.

Next, list your ideal outcomes for your relationship and your family. Do you want to have a new job, live in a different city, have another child, be out of the military in one year? What do you hope your partner is doing in one year? Five years? This exercise will help you identify what your goals are for your relationship, realistic or not. You may decide to change these goals in time, and that will be fine, too.

Lastly, list the strengths of your relationship. What do you do to help resolve problems in your relationship? What values do you share with your partner? What do you appreciate about your partner's efforts since she has returned home from deployment? Be generous to yourself and your partner in this exercise, since despite any disappointments you have had recently, there are definitely bright spots in every relationship that deserve to be noticed.

Clarify Your Fears, Hopes, and Strengths

My Worst Fears:

Example: *The kids won't reconnect with their mother.*

Ideal Outcomes:

Example: *We will settle within thirty minutes from our families.*

Relationship Strengths:

Example: *We have date night at least three times a month.*

Make sure this is a private exercise and not shared with your partner. It is not a list of pros and cons for the relationship, though it may look like this to your partner if she views it. The exercise is meant to make you really think about your mindset, and how your thinking affects your mood and behavior. The goal is to be clear about your thoughts and beliefs and to accept where you are at the moment.

Resuming Intimacy During the Initial Period of Reintegration

Intimacy in couples and families is a broad idea and involves several aspects, including physical, emotional, and sexual intimacy. Also, intimacy manifests differently between different members of the family. Chapter 3 will discuss intimacy in more depth, but here I present some initial suggestions for the first few weeks and months after reunion.

Even though most couples may want to be sexually intimate fairly quickly, this will likely be at least slightly awkward for one or both spouses. It may be even harder for spouses to be emotionally intimate. It is important that you be open to your partner's experiences when you are physically and sexually intimate and be willing to share your feelings about this also. There will likely be many ups and downs as both you and your partner vary between being drawn to one another and wanting distance. In the short term, it is important for both spouses to pay close attention to one another's preferences, especially if you get a sense that these preferences may change from day to day. Sometimes it can be simply letting the other know, "I am not feeling that way right now; let me check in with you later." Frequent and brief conversations may be necessary as each spouse regains comfort with the other early in the reintegration.

Working with your spouse to redevelop her relationship with your children is also important. The key idea here is that the recently deployed parent can accomplish this with frequent, small spans of concentrated time spent with each child. Some literature refers to these as small "dates" between the parent and each child in some activity appropriate for the child. These can be small "islands" of time spent with each child, but in the best of all worlds, they should occur frequently, even daily.

Communication in the Initial Period of Reintegration

Communication about needs and preferences for intimacy was discussed above, and the primary point is that frequent communication should be your primary goal. Remember to set aside enough time to talk with your partner, with no other activities competing for each other's attention. Communication need not always have a particular goal, but it is important to note that talking is really the main vehicle by which we cement our relationships, and it is easy for all the new challenges to prevent you and your partner from just sitting and talking. Try to fit in a chance to do this every day, even if it appears that there is nothing to say.

It is useful to start with a few guidelines for some of the issues that might arise. Your partner may want and need to talk about her deployment experiences, especially if it was a combat deployment. Listen for these moments; it would be less useful to try to force them. If she is reluctant or has not discussed anything with you, you can simply indicate that you are open to hearing about the deployment when she feels like talking about it.

Another guideline is to pay attention to disagreements that become heated and escalate quickly. It is important to develop strategies to defuse these events since they can be emotionally destructive. If you had a way of doing this successfully prior to the deployment, it is worth attempting these same strategies. One spouse I worked with stated, "Our habit was that before anyone said anything nasty to the other, we took ten minutes to cool down, and then we returned to the discussion." Another said, "We had a signal; I let him know using a signal that he was behaving over the top, and he backed off." These are both variants of a method for couples we will discuss called *time-out*. An important point is that returning to the topic after tempers have cooled is a key part of the method.

Final Words

You now know that there are several pathways through the first weeks and months of your reintegration, and that for many couples it is a variable experience. There are several active strategies you can use during this time to begin a successful adjustment. Your limitations as a couple prior to the deployment point to areas to pay particular attention to after the deployment. Use the strategies throughout this book to help you and your partner become a team in confronting these problems. Your expectations and other thoughts about what happens day to day affects how prepared you feel to deal with problems that arise. Use the exercises suggested to clarify what your worries and expectations are, as well as to identify your strengths. Reintegration is an ongoing, active process, and being aware of this will help you make decisions that strengthen your relationship. Frequent communication is the key to redeveloping intimacy and a bond with your partner. Arranging frequent islands of undistracted time between each family member and your partner is a key strategy.

Chapter 3

Rediscovering Intimacy

"I wasn't sure what I should say about what I went through when she was gone. Should I talk about what it is like now that she is back?"

—*Ted*

L earning how to be close again with your partner is a fundamental part of the reintegration process after a military deployment. This chapter focuses on rediscovering your partner and reestablishing intimacy in the months and years after the return from deployment. Intimacy involves emotional, physical, and sexual closeness. It is more than a state of mind; it is a process, based on a series of conversations and other relationship behaviors across many time points. This viewpoint is helpful because you can make choices about the kinds of conversations you try to have with your partner, once you have an idea about what choices you have. This chapter presents what intimacy is, how intimacy is fostered and reestablished, how to understand differences between you and your partner in the desire for intimacy, and how these differences can be managed. I also discuss the role of communication in intimacy and present ways to improve communication with your partner.

Intimacy Basics

Intimacy is one of the most important aspects of relationships. A couple's ability to become close and figure out how much closeness each person wants may be even more important than how much a couple argues. Also, the right amount of closeness with your partner protects your relationship. When there are conflicts in your relationship, the fact that you are close to your partner can prevent these arguments from slowly tearing the relationship apart. During your partner's deployment, the separation between the two of you has been a disruption in intimacy, regardless of how much frequent contact you have had by text, Internet video, or telephone. The next section reviews the nature of intimacy as a way of understanding what you need to regain.

What Is Intimacy?

Most of the definitions of intimacy involve communication: you tell your partner something about your emotions, and then your partner responds by acknowledging the statement in some way. Intimacy is present when your partner responds by expressing understanding, validation, and caring (Reis and Shaver 1988). You might describe your relationship as highly intimate at any given point based on how you are feeling, but this definition makes an important point—your feelings of intimacy are the result of actual communication between you and your partner. Of course, transactions in the other direction, in which your partner speaks and you respond, are also important to your and your partner's feelings of intimacy. How open and expressive and how responsive each of you is probably varies over time. Each time your partner chooses to express an emotion and how you choose to respond can increase intimacy. Are you attentive to what your partner says about how he feels? Do you express caring or communicate that his feelings are real and important, even when they might be difficult to accept? What does your partner do when you express yourself?

Other Forms of Intimacy

Of course, there are other ways to experience and express intimacy, most notably physical intimacy, humor, and playfulness. First, think about how often you share physical contact with your partner. Do you and your partner greet each other with a kiss each morning or when coming and going from the house? How often do you hug? Even without discussing directly how you and your partner are feeling, intimate physical contact on a daily basis is a way to rebuild and retain intimacy between you and your partner.

Likewise, humor and playfulness are important parts of most intimate relationships, and very prominent in most new romantic relationships. Do you and your partner share humor and laugh with one another? How often do you share inside jokes? Can you create new inside jokes? This form of intimacy building is largely based on communication, but as you can imagine, can also be based on nonverbal jokes that you and your partner may share with one another. As you read this chapter, think of the different types of jokes that you and your partner have shared and when you remember engaging in these jokes.

Last, shared activities not primarily involving communication can also facilitate intimacy. These might include goal-oriented tasks (for example, working together on the house or apartment) and leisure, non-goal-oriented activities (such as walking or watching a movie together). A shared positive experience, whether or not it was discussed by you and your partner in any depth, can foster a sense of common purpose and background.

Sexual Intimacy Since Your Partner's Return

Consider how your sexual relationship has redeveloped since your partner returned. It is often the case that sexual intimacy occurred soon after the return of your partner into your home. The frequency of sexual relations, however, may or may not have returned to a comfortable pattern. Chronic pain, particularly from knees, hips, and lower back or more serious combat injuries, is highly common in recent combat veterans and may limit your partner's desire for sexual intimacy. Whether or not you are satisfied with this pattern depends on several factors, including the patterns set prior to your partner's deployment, the degree of stress and conflict each of you are currently feeling, and how close the two of you are feeling emotionally.

This brings up an important point. Emotional intimacy and physical intimacy are usually intertwined, especially in committed relationships. Exactly how they are intertwined differs from person to person. For example, you may feel close after talking about your thoughts and feelings and hearing them accepted; this in turn, may increase your desire for sex and enhance the overall experience of sex. For others, however, being sexual may lead naturally to greater comfort in talking openly about the relationship and about feelings. For still others, emotional and sexual intimacy may occur at more or less the same time. It is helpful to think about what has become the established pattern, or what each of your preferences are, in your relationship now.

Differences in Preferences for Intimacy

Popular culture, including pop psychology, emphasizes differences between men and women, but consider for a moment that these subtle differences between the sexes are often overstated. Many research findings indicate that there are some reliable average differences between men and women on the level of intimacy that males versus females want and experience with others. The situation, however, is much more complex. In research settings, men show that their ability to experience intimacy with close friends is on par with women, but they do not tend to show this in natural situations (Reis, Senchak, and Solomon 1985). It is important to consider, however, that because there are *average* differences between groups of men and women on the experience of intimacy, this difference really is not very big. First, there is a great deal of overlap in how much both men and women want intimacy. The actual *average* differences are rather small compared to the overlap in intimacy (Carothers and Reis 2013). Picture a bell-shaped curve that represents the high and low levels of closeness that women want with their friends. In the middle of this bell-shaped curve, where most women are, are those that want an average amount of intimacy. A similar curve for men would mostly overlap the curve for women, but would just move to the left a small amount. Yes, there is an average difference, but with such a big overlap in the distribution, there are certainly some men in some relationships who want *more* intimacy than the women they are with.

Why do two spouses often seem to be so different? Andy Christensen and Neil Jacobson (2000) write in their book *Reconcilable Differences* about how dissimilarities between spouses can appear to become magnified over time. This process is known as *polarization*. Polarization happens with intimacy in the following way. Imagine you are a spouse who wants to share more feelings and events about the day, and your partner is less comfortable with this. Early in your relationship—which was probably very fresh, new, and fun—it was easy for you and your partner to overlook differences in how much you each wanted to talk at the end of the day. Over time, however, novelty and excitement in relationships usually wears off—often at the same time that relationship stresses, such as raising children, increase. The degree of adjustment you and your partner may be willing to make for the other reduces over time. The more you seek closeness and sharing of your feelings, the less your partner accommodates your attempts and the more your partner begins to avoid or rebuff you. This pattern becomes a very noticeable, self-perpetuating cycle. You attempt to talk about what you are feeling and what has happened during the day, and your partner begs off or tunes out. The more you try to get close, the more your partner draws away, both of you trying to act in a way that is most comfortable. In this way, small initial differences in desire for intimacy are focused on and magnified. You are left with the impression that the differences in what you each want are large;

but in reality, the differences are not much greater than when you first became a couple.

One or more military deployments likely got in the way of having the kind of intimacy that you have come to expect and appreciate. It is typical for service members to hold information about a deployment close for reasons of mission security. They may also do this to prepare themselves mentally for the deployment by turning inward, or in response to the increased demands of training and deployment preparation. The impact of this is often to reduce the opportunities for emotional and physical closeness. Likewise, as mentioned at the outset of the chapter, during the deployment itself, your ability to maintain intimacy compared to before the deployment was limited.

Optimizing Intimacy Using Better Communication

You can use effective communication methods to find the best way to work with your partner to find the level and type of intimacy most comfortable to both of you. A military deployment may actually hasten the decline of intimacy for many couples. Fortunately, one of the opportunities of the reintegration period is the chance to renegotiate the type and degree of intimacy expressed and experienced by you and your partner. Let us next look at the ways in which intimacy can be fostered through communication.

Communication Principles

What are the goals of communication in intimate relationships? There are at least three identifiable goals: emotion-focused sharing, play, and solving problems. Based on the discussion above, you likely have guessed at least the first two of these. For now, we will focus on emotion-focused sharing and play since they are most likely to help with building and managing intimacy in relationships.

Emotion-focused sharing occurs when you talk about your day with your partner, say how you feel about what is happening with the kids, or listen to your partner about how happy he is to be at home with you and the kids. As noted above, this becomes a way to build intimacy when both partners are attentive, responsive, and validating as the other expresses these feelings. Most of the time we are not very direct when sharing how we feel, and this may lead to some problems in getting the best possible response from your partner. You may describe a situation, such as how the kids fought over whether to watch TV or play Xbox, without mentioning directly how frustrated it made you feel. In this example, feeling frustrated or upset is implied and perhaps obvious. Many times, however, our feelings are much more complex and multifaceted. You may not only feel frustrated with the kids but also may feel helpless and alone in trying to figure out how to help them get along better. This additional information may help your partner pay much more attention to what you are saying and respond in a more understanding way.

Another issue that emerges when you share your feelings is that your partner may try to help you solve the problem you are describing. Using the example of your frustration with the kids, your partner may make suggestions about ways you could handle the problem—for example, "Why don't you just tell them they won't get either the TV or the Xbox if they keep fighting?" This may leave you feeling not listened to and invalidated, since the implication is that if you had followed your partner's strategy, you would not feel that way. But if your goal was to feel heard, understood, and supported, your partner's response would leave you unhappy.

Intimacy Communication Guidelines

Several guidelines, which use popular methods for enhancing relationships, can help you enhance your feelings of intimacy with your partner (Accordino and Guerney 2003). Understanding and using these guidelines is possible only if you are very aware of your own communication behavior. Why is this important? You only have direct control over what you choose to say, and your partner may not be following along with these guidelines and has not agreed to try what is suggested. But, you can make many helpful, unilateral changes in how you communicate that will have a tremendous impact on how your partner communicates with you. At the same time, if you make positive changes, it will affect your partner in a way that does not feel as if you are directly attempting to control the conversations in your relationship. Awareness of your own statements will come naturally as you learn more about the different types of statements described here and from watching and listening to yourself as you talk with your partner during your daily life.

Speaker and Listener Roles

First, there are two roles in any conversation, a speaker and a listener, so it is essential for each person to take turns talking. Being a good listener is the most direct way of showing attention and validation of the other's feelings. In most discussions of deep feelings, each person may need at least thirty seconds to two minutes to talk uninterrupted. This may not seem like a long period of time. When asking spouses in a communication training exercise to talk with their partner about their feelings uninterrupted for two minutes, spouses regularly express that it feels like "forever."

There are several strategies you can use when trying to improve turn taking in emotion-focused discussions with your partner. When you feel yourself driven to interrupt in a discussion with your partner, stop yourself and keep listening. You can even pause momentarily after your partner appears to be finished before starting to talk. To encourage your partner to be patient when it is your turn to talk, be as brief as you can. Talk in small paragraphs of two or three sentences. Does this seem like a difficult goal? Start by making slightly briefer statements than is usual for you, gradually disciplining yourself to reduce down to two or three sentences. The impact on your partner will be that he will be less likely to tune out or fear not being able to make his own statement. This occurs because you have demonstrated that your partner does not have to interrupt in order to get a chance to talk.

Focus on Your Partner When Listening

Second, when your partner is speaking, focus on your partner, even when you are not pleased about what you are hearing. Many times service members have unpleasant feelings after returning from a deployment; this may lead to ongoing feelings of anger, irritability, intolerance, or a general sense of lack of feelings. The cause of this can vary from person to person, and grappling with this is an important part of reintegration for many service members and veterans. This can be highly upsetting to hear, as it may lead to fears about your connection between you and your partner. It will be easy to be led by your own internal dialogue about your partner's words, rebutting and denying while potentially missing out on important information. By paying careful attention to your partner's description of his internal feelings, you are enhancing the intimacy and the bond between the two of you, regardless of how upsetting these feelings are.

Summarize Your Partner

Third, briefly summarize your partner's statements whenever possible. This is important in order to let your partner know that you have heard and acknowledge the feelings that your partner is expressing. For example, your partner may say how irritated he has been by people getting upset about small things, and that since he has been back, no one appreciates how tedious day-to-day life is compared to the things he experienced when deployed. A brief summary might be the following: "You're ticked off because people don't get that small things don't matter compared to what you've seen." The key is to reference the emotion that was stated in the original statement along with a brief restatement of the topic that led to the feeling.

Although summaries can be simple, there are several challenges. They may be exceedingly difficult to remember to do because if you find your partner's statements upsetting, the first thing you want to do is to argue against them. It may feel as though providing a summary is agreement that you feel the same way, but actually it is only acknowledgment and validation for your partner that you have heard and understand what he has said. One benefit of a summary is that you do not have to say, "I understand" since by summarizing, you have simply shown it. Providing a summary to a fairly long statement can be a challenge, so you may summarize important parts; this brings up the other benefit of a summary, the fact that the process is self-correcting. Once your partner perceives that you are trying to understand and remember all that was said, he will help out by providing the missing details.

Speak From Your Own Point of View

The fourth guideline is when speaking, speak from your own viewpoint and remember to describe your emotions. You can use the form "when x happens, then I feel y." Some examples include the following: "When we don't get along, I feel upset and separate from you," and "When I see you not talking and not letting me know what is going on, I feel frustrated and sad." In order to help your partner not immediately have a negative reaction to your emotion, you can preface each statement by saying, "I know you look at this differently, but this is how I am feeling about it." This will help you present your thoughts and feelings as your own rather than as the "truth." It is also best to avoid implied blaming statements, such as, "You are making me feel frustrated and sad" as well as very direct and broad blaming statements: "You are causing our relationship problems by not talking to me."

It is also important to connect emotionally by expressing positive feelings. The difficult part of this is to remember to do it. The same guidelines, however, make the effort have more impact. This means identify the situation, event, or behavior, and also name the positive emotion(s) that go along with it. For example, you might say, "Hey, I really loved it when you got down on the floor to play with Jimmy; I feel really close to you when stuff like that is happening."

Things to Avoid

In order to enhance intimacy, there are also things to avoid in this type of conversation. Remember that the goal is to enhance intimacy, rather than to solve problems. Enhancing intimacy can be seen as a way to strengthen the bond between you and your partner. This will make it easier when it is time to generate solutions to the problem at hand. For example, you and your partner may be arguing about how to handle your son, who has begun to get into trouble at school since your partner returned from deployment. It can be helpful to talk about how each person feels about what is happening. You likely have many of the same feelings as your partner, so there is some common ground; in turn, it will help you work against the tendency to blame each other's parenting or the deployment for the difficulty. After this process, it will be easier for each of you to focus on solutions to the problem.

Another tactic to avoid while trying to build intimacy through communication includes trying to make a point or to convince your partner to adopt a certain point of view. You can identify when you are trying to do this by the use of certain phrases, including the following: "Don't you think that…" "But you have to agree that…" "I don't know why you don't admit that…" Each of these phrases often leads to a defensive counter-argument, rather than hearing and accepting your viewpoint. If the goal is greater closeness and sharing, avoid these and similar phrases.

Guiding the Discussion with Your Partner

By following these guidelines you can have more influence on how you and your partner develop closeness through communication. It can be helpful, however, to ask your spouse to collaborate in some of these changes. Usually this means one or two well-placed requests or statements before or during the conversation. For example, to enhance the focus on emotion and sharing, versus solving the problem, you can preface the discussion by saying, "I'd like to say a couple of things about my reactions to our son's trouble at school, and I'd like to hear your reactions; we can talk about how to solve it later." To encourage turn taking, you can say, "Let's talk one at a time, because we both have things to say. Please continue—I'll wait to say something." You can also refocus the discussion from blame to the sharing of emotions in the following way: "I know it's easy for both of us to believe the other is to blame, and I certainly know there are things I could do better; for now I'd like to hear about how you are feeling when our son begins to get on your nerves." Each of these strategies requires you to become a leader, to make an assertive statement, and also to put yourself in the role of the listener as the first step. This type of action can signal to your partner your willingness to draw close by being accommodating in the discussion, letting him know he no longer needs to be on the defensive. This sets a positive tone for the discussion going forward in a similar fashion.

Guidelines for Enhancing Intimacy Through Communication

- **Take turns talking—one speaker and one listener.** Turn taking shows attentiveness and validates your partner's feelings.

- **Focus on the speaker.** When you are listening, pay special attention to your partner's emotions, even when they are unpleasant to hear.

- **Summarize your partner's statements.** By summarizing you demonstrate that you are listening and validating your partner's feelings; it does not mean you necessarily agree or feel exactly the same.

- **Speak from your own point of view.** When you are speaking, focus on your emotions. "When x happens, I feel y."

- **Don't try to solve the problem before talking about your values and feelings about it.** Developing closeness by listening and validating each other's values and feelings is often a necessary prelude to understanding and solving the problem.

- **Avoid trying to make a point.** Trying to convince your partner of a certain viewpoint can work against developing intimacy.

- **Guide the discussion gently if needed.** Ask your partner to take turns talking and let your partner go first; ask your partner to focus on feelings and perceptions first and to solve the problem later.

Renegotiating and Managing Differences in the Desire for Closeness

The reintegration period is a good opportunity to produce shifts in the way you and your partner deal with intimacy in your relationship. Now I want to focus on your choices as you deal with this part of your relationship. One of those choices is when and how to attempt to bring your partner closer through talking or other things you might do together, which we will call a "bid." Making a bid requires some risk, being honest with yourself about what it is you want from your partner, and also being willing to accept what your partner is able to provide at that particular time.

Bids for Intimacy

When you are making an attempt to bring your partner closer, you are making a bid (Gottman and DeClaire 2001). Much like the commonplace concept of a bid, a bid for emotional closeness can be accepted or not. A bid can be expressed as a proposal—"Hey, let's go for a walk"—or as a request, such as, "Can I talk to you about something important?" Other bids are nonverbal in nature, such as pulling your partner close for a kiss or hug, an affectionate pat on the backside, or looking at your partner with "that look" and gesturing toward the bed. As you might imagine, spouses in happy relationships are much more likely to accept bids for emotional connection than those in unhappy relationships. Also, if a particular bid is not accepted, in happy relationships spouses rebid relatively soon in a small fraction of cases, but in unhappy relationships, spouses will rarely rebid once the bid is refused.

There are several strategies that will make your bids for increased closeness most successful. First, present the acceptance of a bid as a choice. An example might be, "I'd love to have a cup of coffee with you if you're feeling like it." Also important is that acceptance of the bid is not limited to a narrow slice of time—give your partner some wiggle room. This offers your partner the choice of not turning away from your bid for emotional closeness while at the same time declining the immediate proposal. An example of this strategy might be, "I'd love to have a cup of coffee with you if you're feeling like it. If now is not good, maybe we can catch something later." This provides some options without letting go of your general message that you would like to connect.

Second, make sure your bids do not have threats or strings attached. For example, try to avoid "Let's go get a cup of coffee—you know, we never do that anymore." There is high temptation to point out in the bid that your partner has come up short in the past regarding your offers—but this has the effect of creating guilt and a sense of obligation. If your partner accepts, both of you may wonder whether it was done out of duty or in response to mild coercion rather than under free will. If your partner refuses, it may be hard to tell whether this reflects a lack of desire, an attempt to resist your coercion, or a demonstration of the desire to be independent of your influence.

Last, you can increase your opportunities for success in bids for closeness by accepting as many of your partner's bids as possible. When you cannot accept the specific bid, avoid turning away from the bid and offer an alternative time. Using the example in which your partner makes an offer to get a cup of coffee, you could respond in the following way: "I really would like to, but I was just headed out to get the groceries. I'd like to do it later—will that work?" A similar response that is a clear rejection of the bid might sound like the following: "You know I'm heading out to get groceries."

Your Role in Facilitating Reintegration

As the partner who did not deploy, you can play a crucial role in family reintegration by being willing to make more bids for intimacy than your partner. One of the most common experiences of service members and their spouses after a deployment is a sense of disconnection from others in their family and their social network. After deployment, veterans may report feeling like guests in their own homes (Sayers et al. 2009). You in turn likely feel that your partner is withdrawing from you. But it's probably much harder for your partner to reach out to you for intimate connection than it is for you to reach out to him, so making the bids yourself will be helpful.

This leads to several questions the spouse of a returning service member may face. First, there is the question of whether it's fair that you feel that you are making more and repeated bids to increase the closeness between the two of you. It may be helpful to consider that you and your partner have different roles in this process. Your deployed partner endured a difficult process of personal transformation through training, being deployed, and returning. And though your increased home responsibilities as the partner not deployed may have led to changes for you also, the transition back from deployment is arguably greater for your partner. One of the important roles you can play in the process is to provide regular opportunities for your partner to respond to bids for greater intimacy, as well as to be highly aware of bids for intimacy made by your partner.

Second, how do you manage to provide bids for intimacy in a positive way when you may be feeling that a great deal of emotional intimacy is missing? As discussed above, it is best when bids do not refer to lost opportunities, but sometimes you will have to let your partner know about the closeness that you need. The key is to make sure that you make bids for spending time together separate from those meant to convey your feelings of unhappiness. Therefore, one bid for positive time spent together may be the following: "I'd love for us to go out for a meal this Friday." The other bid, which expresses discontent, might sound like the following: "I need to tell you that I am really missing talking in the evenings like we used to; I know you may not like hearing this, but it is something I need you to know." It is fine to present both types of bids, but just remember to deliver them at different times. The main reason for this is that the second type of bid requires very little response from the partner, since it does not actually ask for immediate action but is an honest expression of emotion.

The third question you might face is, for how long does one continue to make bids that are not accepted? Are you concerned you will have to wait months or years? The answer to this question varies from person to person of course. Each person must determine her own degree of tolerance for a relationship in which the needs for intimacy are not met. Some spouses will feel that the military veteran in their relationship is withdrawing and focusing inward, and has fewer personal resources to express and experience intimacy. This may be the result of the emotional and physical effects of exposure to combat experiences. If this is the case, seeking mental health treatment or physical rehabilitation for the veteran may be helpful.

Managing Intimacy Needs in Your Relationship

Because differences in intimacy needs are reasonably common, we can focus on this issue first. There are several strategies for managing differences in preferences for emotional and physical intimacy between partners. First, to some extent, it is best for a spouse of a service member or veteran not to attempt to blame these differences directly on military service, on deployment, or specifically on combat operations. Although these experiences are quite possibly important factors, discussions about the origin of such differences can become the focus of arguments with your partner, leaving you both with less energy to devote to managing the differences themselves. Your partner may see his preference as an individual choice, rather than as a result of the impact of military service.

Second, using the reintegration period as a new start, you and your partner can work on becoming more skilled at gracefully deferring each other's bids for intimacy when the time is not right. After all, even if two spouses are generally perfectly matched on how much emotional and physical closeness they want, there will always be specific times when one partner's need for closeness is not felt by the other. Dealing with these mismatches in a gentle way is a skill that you and your partner can learn and become expert at over time.

Third, many of our human needs for intimacy also can be met through friendships. This can be an important way to deal with the need for connection and expression of your thoughts and feelings when you are lacking this in your relationship with your partner. That does not mean that everything you want to discuss with your partner will be fair game for discussions with your best friend; instead, it is important to establish a connection with your friend around the interests and topics that are shared mutually with that friend. For example, if your partner does not want to join you on activities outside the house, this is a perfect opportunity to develop a relationship with a friend who has similar interests, whether it is hiking, volunteer work, or a book group. In the beginning of this chapter, I raised the question of how and when you and your partner experienced playfulness and humor. An essential skill in the redevelopment of intimacy in your relationship is to create the opportunities for renewing your and your partner's experience of playfulness. A portion of your bids can focus on creating time spent together with very low task demands and very low expectations. For example, you can ask your partner to make a regular time during the week to spend time on a shared activity—game night, movie night, or a regular walk—and the exact activity depends on your history together. The goal is to create a time and space in which a mutually enjoyable, pleasant time could be made a regular expectation of the week.

Making these suggestions may place you at risk of some of your bids being refused. But, as stated above, it may be important to give your partner multiple opportunities to accept them. It will allow him plenty of choices and increases the overall chances of redeveloping intimacy in your relationship as part of reintegration.

Final Words

Redeveloping intimacy is an important part of family reintegration for deployed service members and their partners, and it presents a new opportunity to reset the direction of the relationship. Intimacy is primarily developed through communication, and your communication choices can make a great deal of difference in how and whether intimacy is regained in your relationship. Your and your partner's feelings of intimacy depend on whether each of you respond and validate one another when you each express emotions. You can help increase the degree of emotions expressed in several ways: by being an attentive listener; by taking turns as a listener and speaker in emotion-focused conversations; by summarizing the feelings in your partner's statements; by focusing on expressing emotions instead of convincing your partner of your point of view; and by sharing your emotions about a problem before trying to solve it. You can improve your communication with your partner by providing good examples of communication and by making well-phrased suggestions about the direction of the conversation. Bids for intimacy are important steps in creating the opportunity for an emotionally intimate exchange. And bids are most successful when they provide options for when they can be accepted and do not have strings attached. When you accept as many bids from your partner as you can, you increase the chances that your partner will accept your bids. Although it may be easy to attribute differences in desires for intimacy in your relationship to your partner's military service, differences in these preferences exist in nearly every relationship at some point in time. Greater awareness of kind and skillful ways to manage the level of intimacy in your relationship will greatly enhance your relationship satisfaction.

Chapter 4

Who Does What?

"I could not seem to get him to talk about the budget. He would just spend money without looking at our account and then claim I was trying to control our money when I got mad."

—*Alicia*

"Things settled in just like before—we pretty much shared responsibilities—except I continued paying the bills, which I was doing while she was away."

—*Jamal*

R eactions to the return of a relationship partner can vary widely. Some couples develop a smooth way of adjusting to this change; others fight over the division of responsibilities, which becomes an ongoing source of stress. This chapter will discuss the factors that make the division of responsibilities and decision making difficult for couples reintegrating after a deployment. In addition, I will describe ways to negotiate changes in household roles and responsibilities.

Factors in Household Roles

Several underlying themes are important in the discussion about the division of responsibilities in relationships. The roles each person has in an intimate relationship and how partners make decisions about roles are intertwined with struggles over control and influence in the relationship. Each partner may also have very clear ideas about what is right for him or her to do, based on male and female gender roles. All of these factors can make reintegrating after deployment more complicated. I will start with a discussion of general trends in American household roles and how they are affected by the deployment cycle.

Changes in Household Roles

For decades in the United States, there has been a general trend for women to join the workforce, resulting in a larger proportion of dual-earner households and a shift toward more flexibly defined roles for men and women in families. These changes are also present in military couples, even with the employment challenges for spouses of service members due to frequent relocations. Those who serve in the reserve or National Guard component of the military may depend even more upon the income of the partner not serving in the military; and if that partner is female, she is likely to handle more of the household responsibilities than the male partner. To understand what types of roles and household responsibilities you want now, think about how your household roles have evolved over time. Also, think about how you managed all of the household roles and responsibilities when your partner was deployed.

When your partner returned from deployment, what types of shifts occurred? You may have argued with your partner about goals and methods of handling money. Your partner may want to resist how you handled spending and bills and make separate decisions about spending that do not fit with decisions you have made. Alternatively, you may get caught up in frequent arguments: about how much each of you contributes to the daily household responsibilities, which of you cares more often for the children, and whether or not it matters how often the car is washed. Although before your partner's deployment you may have had a system worked out, factors like your partner's new focus on changing careers or nagging concerns about chronic medical problems stemming from combat may well have changed that system.

Autonomy, Control, and Influence in Relationships

There are several factors constantly at work in most long-term relationships that can produce conflict during a time of transition such as reintegration after a military deployment. The need for autonomy is a basic human desire that motivates many of our activities, even in close relationships (Ryan and Deci 2000). Autonomy can be defined as having independent thoughts, feelings, and preferences. In a way similar to intimacy, each partner has his and her own preference for the degree of autonomy needed within the relationship, and these differences may be a source of ongoing arguments (Christensen and Jacobson 2000). In fact, although they are not technically opposites, autonomy and intimacy represent two human needs that can work in opposition to one another. The more your partner acts autonomously, the less intimacy may be fostered. Imagine, for example, that your partner wants to buy a specific cell phone. The more you express your thoughts and feelings about the matter, the more it may in fact lead her to feel as though she's forced to take your wishes into account. And, because of your partner's need to make her own decisions—that is, to act autonomously—she may act contrary to your opinions, leading to a heated argument. In this way, her need for autonomy overwhelmed her need for intimacy. The topic of spending in this disagreement is not as important as the struggle over it; you may argue just as much about who will pay the electric bill as who spends time with the kids on Saturday afternoon. You may have heard yourself, or your partner, complain, "Why do you always try to make me do it your way?" This complaint may be expressing the feeling that one partner is encroaching on the other's autonomy.

Many spouses experience this type of conflict as a control struggle. Although you may not understand it this way at first, when we feel that we have fewer options and less control, we actually tend to behave in a more controlling manner. When you see your partner acting in a way that appears to limit your influence in a situation, you may react by trying to gain more influence and control yourself. The trouble with this is that as both partners react in the same way, the conflict increases. Both you and your partner are attempting to exert control and influence, which leads to still more attempts to exert influence and control by the other. The practical result can be twofold—repeated arguments about what and how things are to be done and an increasing number of decisions and actions taken by each partner without consulting the other partner.

Attempts to Influence in Relationships: Strategies and Goals

It is helpful for you to improve your ability to observe both your own and your partner's ways of influencing each other in the relationship. As an exercise, think about the last time you and your partner discussed a practical family problem, such as how to get a particular bill paid or how to get the car serviced. How did you each approach the discussion? Did you state what you wanted to happen and provide some reasons? Did your partner propose another way for the task to get done, and then did the two of you argue about whether this would work?

Making a logical argument about the merits of a particular solution is one of the most common strategies couples use. For example, your partner may say that she believes you should continue managing the checkbook because her deployments, training, and other military commitments may cause her to miss paying bills, which would hurt both of you. Furthermore, she states it is something she is "not very good at." In another example, you might argue that your partner "should take the car to get serviced because you are way too busy."

Most attempts at influence in human relationships have multiple goals behind them (Wilson 2002). There are two goals underlying each of the arguments presented above that might not be immediately clear. In the first example regarding the checkbook, your partner's goal is to convince you to continue handling the checkbook and bill paying. There is an additional goal, however; your partner also wants to preserve the strength of your relationship by putting the argument in a positive way—it is good for the relationship to ensure consistent bill paying and also to acknowledge your skills. In the second example, you are arguing that your partner should take the car to get serviced, with the subtext being that your partner is less busy or that you are bearing a greater burden within the relationship. The additional goal is toward getting your partner to accept and confirm your view of yourself as working harder than your partner on family tasks. Unfortunately, this is a somewhat negative argument that tends to place your partner in a bad light. Additional types of influence attempts that erode your bond with your partner include threats and demands ("Do it this way or else!" and "This is the only way acceptable to me!"). Besides the goal of trying to be convincing, the implicit goal behind these types of statements is to show how powerful and resolved we are by limiting the choices of our partner. Most of the time when we use these statements, we are really feeling the opposite of powerful and resolved.

Skilled and Unskilled Examples of Influence Attempts and Their Underlying Goals

"I'd like you continue paying the bills—my schedule may make me miss payments, and you are really organized with it." *(Skilled)*

- Convince the partner to continue a task

- Emphasize the importance of the relationship

- Express appreciation for the skills of the partner

"I really don't have time to do the bills; can't you do them?" *(Unskilled)*

- Convince the partner to continue a task

- Convince the partner that the speaker works harder than the partner

"Just *do* the bills; it's the only way it'll work." *(Unskilled)*

- Force the partner to continue a task
- Demonstrate resolve and power

There are better alternatives when trying to gain cooperation from your partner than with statements that inherently undermine your relationship. Because all of us have a need for some level of autonomy, the way out of this trap is to acknowledge this autonomy in a concrete way. The best way of doing this is by presenting the problem as a common goal and gaining the collaboration of your partner toward this goal, rather than being concerned primarily that your partner accept your solution. In addition, it is important that solutions are presented as meaningful possibilities in which your partner has a clear choice. This will stimulate many better possible solutions to the problem, and your partner's autonomy is acknowledged.

Some examples of engaging your partner on a problem, while clearly acknowledging your partner's autonomy, include the following: "I think we need a better way to get the car into the shop since it really needs some work. I have some ideas. I know you have some ideas, so let's try to come up with some solutions that both of us are willing to try." Another example might be: "I'd like to hear some of your thoughts also about how to get the car serviced." These examples illustrate the basic theme of the message and usually would be part of a conversation rather than a single statement or two.

Suggestions for Negotiating Roles and Routines

Many couples let the roles and routines that occur in their family evolve without discussion, but this does not necessarily lead to the best habits as a family. Consider the steps described below as a way to work with your partner to shift your patterns as a couple and family in a way that works better for everyone.

Weekly Couple's "Business" Meetings

Having a weekly business meeting with your partner is a decidedly unromantic idea, but weekly meetings can actually help you improve the romantic aspects of your relationship. The idea behind the weekly business meeting is to help you and your partner deal with the week-to-week issues such as family schedules and bills and to make it easier to set aside other positive time spent with your partner. Dealing regularly with these issues will prevent the development of larger problems, such as a past-due bill or scheduling conflicts that occur because of other commitments. When conflicts about these issues are dealt with early on and contained within the business meeting, there is less chance that these issues will intrude upon other, more pleasurable leisure time spent together.

The ideal structure of a business meeting is simple, and a few guidelines will help you avoid many of the common pitfalls. In order to be effective, business meetings need to be regular and expected so they occur at roughly the same time each week. To accommodate weekly fluctuations in availability for you and your partner, it is important to identify a secondary time for the meeting to occur. The meeting can be from twenty minutes to an hour, with the more common time being about twenty to thirty minutes. This is important in creating the sense that each weekly meeting is substantial enough to set aside time to make sure it happens but short enough not to intrude into the daily schedule. Each meeting is friendly but task oriented, so emotionally oriented conversations focused on encouraging closeness are limited. The majority of the meeting is not meant to be spent on discussing an argument that occurred that week. From time to time it will be necessary to discuss preferences and feelings about a decision. This can be handled in the way described below.

Each weekly meeting should have an agenda involving some or all of the following topics: individual and family schedules (including leisure activities), payment of bills, routine household tasks, and identification of long-term planning issues. Ideally, desired changes in household tasks are addressed within the context of weekly business meetings. But if changes in how household tasks are accomplished become an area of frequent disagreement, then a discussion of this topic might be handled in a separate conversation. Handling a more controversial issue this way prevents the weekly meeting from becoming tense on a regular basis and something that you or your spouse quickly starts to avoid.

How do you implement the weekly business meeting with your partner if she is not following along in this book? First, the best way to involve your partner is to present the concept of a regular meeting with plenty of options about when and how it is handled. For example, "When is a good time to sit down and talk about the bills and the rest of what we need to do? I would like for us to both be aware of the schedule and make sure we don't miss any due dates." After a brief and successful meeting, you might then suggest that it be a weekly event. If you believe that your partner may be less willing to be regularly involved in working through the schedule, then you can shoulder the initial responsibility of gathering all the information in the following way: "I'd like to talk over how we are working on the bills; when would be a good evening for us to go over them for about twenty minutes each week?" Second, the guidelines presented above can be the goal, as opposed to the rule for each session. The only fairly important guidelines to try to stick to early on, in developing this relationship routine, are that the meetings be relatively brief (twenty to thirty minutes) and occur regularly.

There are several potential pitfalls in planning to have weekly meetings with your partner. For most couples, making the meetings routine can be the biggest difficulty. Regularity can be promoted by providing a consistent prompt, such as, "Tonight after dinner we were going to meet about the bills and schedule—is that still going to work?" In order to maximize your partner's contribution and prevent avoidance, it may be helpful to ask every so often about the routine time and whether your partner would rather pick a different time. Another pitfall is that your partner may feel that you are controlling the relationship decisions because you frequently promote weekly meetings, and she may want to disengage as a way to resist your influence. To demonstrate that your partner has control and influence in the relationship, you can communicate this by indicating your desire for your partner's input. You can say, for example, "I'd like us to meet because I need your input. I shouldn't make these decisions alone; I think we need to make them together." In addition, you can indicate your flexibility by accepting your partner's ideas about how to proceed on an issue. As discussed below regarding problem solving, no solution is set in stone; each solution should be evaluated to see how it is working, so the solutions you agree to can be addressed in a future meeting if they are unsatisfactory. Last, couples can also get sidetracked in recurring relationship disagreements. The communication guidelines presented below can be helpful in avoiding this pitfall and having the most productive discussions possible.

Communication Guidelines

As I discussed in chapter 3, there are three primary goals for communication in intimate relationships: emotion-focused sharing, play, and problem solving. Problem solving is the predominant mode of communication that facilitates the negotiation of roles and routines. Fortunately, there are many problem-solving guidelines and styles for the weekly business meetings and more focused problem solving. The main principle is to remain task oriented as much as possible. In cases involving a great deal of disagreement and bad feelings that require a solution, a short-term solution can be sought with time set aside at some future point to explore the feelings around the topic.

Communication During Weekly Business Meetings

As stated above, the weekly meeting is best driven by an agenda that includes recurrent items such as scheduling of weekly tasks, appointments, leisure time, bills, chores, and identification of longer term planning issues. The communication that you use during these meetings is actually an informal style of problem solving. Several general guidelines make the process more effective.

Guidelines for Better Communication During Weekly Couple's Business Meetings

- **Meetings are regular, last twenty to sixty minutes, are task oriented, and occur at about the same time each week.** It is important to build good meeting habits through regular meetings that are successful, efficient, and productive.

- **Follow an agenda of items to be discussed.** Make a list of agenda items throughout the week, and ask your partner to do the same; items can include family and individual scheduling, routine bills, household chores, and raising topics for long-term planning.

- **Take turns talking.** Taking turns ensures both partners get a say and feel heard, and it reduces tension in the conversation.

- **Summarize the proposal and make a note of the plan.** Repeating what solution is being considered will prevent many misunderstandings.

- **Stay on topic.** Remain mindful about what agenda item is being discussed and be willing to gently guide the conversation back to the topic.

- **Discuss specifics.** Make sure that what is decided is specific enough for the situation.

- **Acknowledge your partner's independence and autonomy.** Recognize that your partner likely has different but valid ways of thinking about the issue, even when this is hard to see in the midst of the discussion.

- **Avoid blaming and name calling.** It is best not to bog the conversation down by implying that your partner is to blame for the occurrence of the problem; using labels and phrases like "careless with money" or "uptight" will make your partner angry and defensive.

- **Avoid dwelling on past occurrences of the issue or problem.** Disagreement between spouses' memories of events is highly common and considered normal.

First, it is best to assemble an agenda before the meeting. You can start in the days or hours ahead of the meeting time by saying, "Tonight I think we need to talk about the schedule of doctors' appointments for the kids, what we are doing this weekend, and the bills to be paid. What else do you think we should put on the list?" If you are leading the effort to start weekly business meetings, you might create a list on a spiral-bound pad or a shared online calendar or to-do list, and ask your partner to contribute to it, using the request suggested above. Be flexible if your partner has a different preference for creating this list, since gaining your partner's engagement in the process is the most important goal.

Once you sit down with your partner, remember to take turns speaking and listening to your partner. If you tend to be more talkative, remember to give your partner some breathing room in between one statement and the next without interjecting quickly. This has the effect of reducing the tension and quick emotional reactions that can easily arise during discussion of thorny issues. If you're generally more of a listener, it may be useful to push yourself to provide more ideas and feedback than usual. Providing a summary can help clarify what is being discussed.

Another important guideline is to stay on topic. This requires some mindfulness during the meeting on your part as well as a willingness to provide a gentle reminder for both of you to stay on track. You can use a statement similar to the following: "That's another good topic to add to the list; let's finish deciding about the schedule this weekend and then turn to that." Also, it is most helpful to be specific in your discussions about solutions to the issues that are discussed. Although this can certainly be taken to extremes and frustrate your partner, there are times when specificity means the difference between a successful or unsuccessful plan. For example, when attempting to work out transportation for the kids' sports events during the weekend, it is highly important to know exactly what time your son's and daughter's games are scheduled. Or, if you discuss a plan for dividing up household chores, it may be important to mention what rooms would be cleaned and in what manner.

While generating ideas about a scheduling issue or a solution, again, it is important to acknowledge your partner's need for autonomy and independence of viewpoint. That is, your partner will likely want something different than what you want, and need to contribute different information and thoughts to the process. Aside from hearing your partner's ideas about the topic at hand, ensure that you demonstrate some give-and-take. It is important that you recognize that your partner's views are different from yours and they have validity even when it is hard to see this while you are in the midst of the discussion. It is not necessary to try to get your partner to agree to your favored solution to each problem or task that is discussed. Rarely is any problem so crucial that showing flexibility and trying one of your partner's ideas is going to lead to disaster. Showing flexibility often leads to greater flexibility from your partner over time.

There are several types of communications that are important to avoid. Blaming often occurs in the context of describing one's idea of why things did not work out well previously. Avoiding blame can help lead you and your partner away from an ineffective and unpleasant discussion about the tasks and responsibilities that you face. Blaming can be direct; but more often, it is implied in the way we describe the problem. For example, you might say, "Last weekend, when you took the car to the store in the afternoon, I was left without a car to take the kids to sports." Implying that your partner's taking the car was the cause of the transportation problem, rather than miscommunication about schedules, will lead your partner to be defensive and to react with anger. A similar type of communication is name calling. Even referring to your partner as uptight or lazy ("You're just being uptight") is enough to derail a productive conversation.

Another type of communication to avoid is focusing on the past history of the task or problem at hand. Focusing on the past can often lead to extended discussions about conflicting memories of events that are difficult or impossible to reconcile. It is not uncommon for spouses to assume that because they experienced the same event, their memories of that event should also be exactly the same. Furthermore, spouses often assume that agreeing on the details of what happened in the past regarding an issue is a crucial step to producing a better plan. Neither of these assumptions is correct. Our memories are usually faulty and biased toward the aspects that are important to each of us as individuals; this is common, and it is considered normal among spouses. You only need to agree upon a general outline of the occurrence of the problem in order to produce a new workable solution or plan.

Problem-Solving Steps for Addressing Household Roles

Some problems require more formal problem-solving methods because they are complex, are particularly challenging, or may be based on recurring conflicts in style or preferred solutions. Often, your partner is not only reintegrating into the family after a deployment; she may also be launching a new career after leaving active military service, beginning school, or both. At the same time, you may be continuing to work or may also be in school. Perhaps the two of you are raising small children after relocating to a new area away from family support. New patterns of work and home roles will likely be required, and you may experience conflict with your partner as you try to work through these changes. A problem I have seen in many couples in the postdeployment period concerns dealing with child care while the veteran is going to school—each spouse understands the need for both the nonmilitary spouse to work and for the veteran to go to school to advance her overall income-generating potential.

Below are a set of steps that can be helpful in providing more structure to the problem-solving process. As stated above, for particularly recurrent and conflict-ridden topics, negotiate with your partner about setting aside some additional time other than your weekly meeting to discuss these difficult issues. Listed below are the basic problem-solving steps:

- Define the problem.

- Generate solutions.

- Combine solutions to create a plan.

- Use a trial period to evaluate the plan.

Define the Problem. Problem-solving steps may be well-known to each of you as an individual process, but some adaptations are necessary for couples. First, it is important to define the problem and write this definition down when it is agreed upon. Problem-solving success is often determined by how the problem is defined. Problem definitions need to be described mutually and with fairness to both partners. When a problem is defined as "Robin has not found the time to get the grocery shopping done regularly," the process is doomed because it implies that the situation is Robin's fault and narrows the possible solutions needlessly. A mutual definition of the problem might be the following: "Because of our busy schedules, we have difficulty getting the grocery shopping done regularly." This does not hide the issues that complicate the matter, but simply does not refer to who typically bought groceries or which partner might have greater flexibility in his or her schedule. Be willing to separate problems if at all possible. An overly broad definition of the problem might refer to all chores; this may also fail because there are too many details to work through at one time, and most chores can be discussed separately.

Generate solutions. The second step is to generate as many usable solutions as possible. One useful trick is to use a couples-based brainstorming method. This method involves each person generating as many solutions as possible, without any evaluation at all, as rapidly as they can. This process can be fun and creative, especially if you are disciplined about avoiding evaluation of the solutions (in other words, avoid saying, "No, that won't work!") and allow yourself to generate humorous and unworkable solutions at the same time. The more solutions, the better, and the more humor, the more creative and open each of you become. You can illustrate this method to your partner, for example, by explaining the concept behind it in order to get her participation or by asking your partner to read about brainstorming here or elsewhere. In any event, it is important to try to write down all of the solutions as you and your partner generate them. Continue for at least five minutes, although for difficult problems, longer or multiple brainstorming sessions can be useful. Try to collect fifteen to twenty-five solutions, although many solutions may be similar or related to one another.

Create a plan. In the third step, you discuss, select, and create a plan for the problem. Typically, each spouse can select and combine a set of the solutions in turn. Creating a plan takes a good deal of give-and-take and discussion. The focus should be on making proposals rather than criticizing your partner's proposals. It is important that while you propose a plan, include solutions generated by your partner whenever possible. This lends a great deal of goodwill to the process, and your partner will learn to do the same over time. If you and your partner get stuck, you might present the idea that any solution can be considered a temporary attempt; if it does not work to the overall satisfaction of both partners, then another plan can be tried.

Set a trial period. In the fourth step you and your partner set a trial period. As noted above, this is an extremely important part of the process. Without testing out solutions and without the understanding that any solution can be altered as needed, it is difficult to generate flexibility and the willingness to try out any plan that you personally did not generate. The length of the trial period is always related to the problem, and the length of the test depends on how much time is needed to know whether the plan worked. At the end of the trial period, progress is reviewed, and then the process can start again at the first step when necessary.

Here is an example of how Trish and Andy solved a complex problem. They were in the second year after Andy returned from deployment and the first year after he separated from active duty. Andy and Trish did not have enough money for bills some months, even though Andy was working at a part-time security job while taking classes. Trish was working a reduced three-days-a-week schedule as a nurse but was feeling burdened in caring for the kids during the week and many weekends because of Andy's security job. They were not very satisfied with the child-care situation and were thinking about taking their kids out of day care. They were arguing because it would make things worse in the short term if Trish did not work, and it would hinder them financially in the long run if Andy did not continue with school and stayed at home with the kids instead. Trish did not want to work full-time since she felt that it was important to spend more time with the kids in their current stages of development, but she felt Andy's part-time work meant they never had time as a family and she never had much of a break from the kids when she was at home.

In the problem-definition stage, they narrowed down the problem to the financial aspect and set aside the child-care problem until later. They defined the problem as follows: "We do not have enough money for bills with income from only our part-time work." They stated it briefly this way because they each had concerns about the other denying them the activity important to them (staying in school, working part-time to be with the kids). During the brainstorming phase, they generated eighteen solutions, including the following: Trish moves to full-time work, allowing Andy to quit the weekend work; Andy cuts back his classes to one per semester; Andy gets a better paying security job; they move to Virginia to stay on Trish's parents' farm; Trish does emergency department work for three twelve-hour shifts during the month; they get rid of the dog to save expenses; and they take on a roommate to help pay the rent. Some of the solutions were unacceptable and not helpful (getting rid of the dog) or ridiculous and humorous (moving to Trish's parents' farm). However, they were able to see the range of combinations that would help them improve their financial situation and came up with a compromise to try for a few months. Trish agreed to add in three or four twelve-hour emergency department shifts per month (which was easy work for her to get), and Andy would quit his part-time security job. Trish's additional shifts generated greater income than Andy's low-paying security job. This shifted the parenting responsibility to Andy on the weekends, which he was willing to do.

The most important aspect of their solving the problem was that they were able to create some trust in each other that each would work toward the common goal of more income while preserving each other's personal goals as much as possible. Furthermore, if the solution did not work well enough for one or both of them, they could try a different combination. They used the problem-solving steps in sequence and the communication guidelines to avoid blaming or using derogatory names for each other, to stay on topic, and to develop a reasonable and detailed plan to try.

Final Words

Reintegration from a military deployment involves resetting the patterns in work and home roles and provides an opportunity to rethink the best way for a couple to arrange their lives together. How partners renegotiate these roles is affected by the specific ways that each person attempts to discuss and influence his or her partner around these issues. At times, it is easy to attempt these changes in ways that threaten your partner's need to have independent thoughts, feelings, and preferences rather than encouraging him or her to work with you on this challenge. Setting up a weekly business meeting is an important step in developing a positive, effective working partnership around the "business" of intimate relationships. Task-oriented and respectful communication methods are important for successful meetings. At times, the use of formal problem-solving steps is necessary to solve challenging problems related to schedules and responsibilities in your household.

Chapter 5

Watching

"I started being really aware of how he was around the house—I could tell he had changed, and I wasn't sure what he was going to react to or when he would just be silent."

—*Trish*

"For a while, I had to pay close attention to how she talked to the kids. Sometimes she would really be harsh, and she had everyone walking on eggshells."

—*Evan*

As the result of military training and deployment experiences, your partner may have developed a sense of overprotectiveness of you and your family, may often be quiet and withdrawn, or frequently may seem irritable. This may make you start watching closely how your partner talks with you or your children, and it may have a negative effect on the general mood of all family members. Conversations about these reactions can also lead to arguments. One spouse with whom I worked stated, "I gave him a hard time for swerving around a bag when driving in a parking lot, laughed, and said 'What is the big problem? It's just a paper bag.'" This led to a loud verbal fight in which the service member partner stressed that the bag could hide explosives and the spouse countered by arguing how unlikely this was.

This chapter will describe the impact of training and deployment on service members and veterans using ideas developed first by mental health experts in the US Army in a program called Battlemind (Adler et al. 2009). The program was developed to help deployed service members understand the impact of these training and deployment experiences on their thinking and behavior and then make the adjustment to civilian life. I will review some of the concepts behind this program to help you understand better why your partner acts the way he does. The last part of this chapter will present several ways to cope with and work with your partner on adjusting to these issues in your relationship.

The Impact of Military Training and Deployment Experiences on Individuals and Relationships

Military training leaves a permanent imprint on individuals who join military service. Training is continuous and involves significant hardship and a great deal of hard work. It entails learning both new skills that are useful in a broad range of situations and some that are useful in a very narrow set of circumstances, such as combat. Deployments also leave an imprint on service members, but the impact is much less predictable. Below I describe some of the aspects of military training and deployment that may stay with a service member past the return from deployment.

Ways of Thinking and Resulting Behaviors

There are several aspects of military training and deployment that are associated with the ways of thinking discussed in the Battlemind program, and the most common are described below. The impact of training and deployment and the reactions they lead to are very common, and even expected, in all service members who are deployed. These reactions to training and deployment tend to change over time, but you and your partner can actively work better together through these changes so they do not have as much of an effect on your relationship.

Withholding Information

As you are aware, the military generally operates on a need-to-know principle, and deployments involve even greater expectations of OPSEC, or operations security. You may expect that the intimacy you developed with your partner prior to the deployment may qualify you as part of those who need to know, but service members are instructed that this is not the case. For many service members, this way of thinking may become habitual and extend to feelings and personal whereabouts even after the deployment has ended. For example, you might find that your partner leaves the house without telling you where he is going or does not inform or discuss important decisions with you, such as choices of jobs or schools after retiring from military service. One spouse I interviewed discovered that her husband had decided to reenlist, but she learned this only when the orders that he was to report soon for predeployment training were delivered to the house. Also, your partner built bonds during the deployment, and you may feel that he does not share feelings with you as often and wants to spend more time with those in his old unit than with your family.

Irritability, Aggression, and Suppressing Emotions

The way your partner handles emotions may confuse and upset you, and it may be unclear how training and deployment experiences could continue to affect your partner long after returning from deployment. Training and combat experiences dramatically influence how your partner has learned aggressive attitudes and the use of aggressive behaviors in certain situations. Quick and decisive action is required as a way to survive. Controlling the enemy, using deadly force when necessary, and quick, defensive actions are all part of training and extend through the most technical of strategic actions. The use of aggression and anger are targeted toward the enemy, and many service members learn to suppress, control, and ignore other emotions. Emotions may be thought of as a tool, rather than as the spontaneous reaction that most of us experience them to be. The physical feelings "in the gut" that people usually experience as emotion may be denied as having anything to do with emotion.

Even when you see your partner quickly responding with irritability, your partner may deny feeling emotions about many important events and even anger. One former army service member I worked with often insisted that he was not angry. He stated that when he loudly confronted his teenage son, it was his way of demanding respect and getting results from him, not a sign of anger. His wife, of course, was frightened that their son might respond physically and thought a softer approach would be much more effective. But she could not understand how her partner could deny feeling angry at their son because the son actually did show disrespect.

Another couple I knew also illustrates the common problem of irritability. Colin, a veteran of three deployments to Iraq, no longer enjoyed parties and large cookouts that the couple had often attended and also hosted with neighborhood friends. Julia, his wife, would often ask him to go with her and their two children during the summer to several cookouts and outside parties. When asked, he complained about the heat, the "idiots" who continually asked him about his deployments to Iraq, and the drinking that led others to become "loud and obnoxious." He angrily told her to stop asking and stated that by refusing to go he was just making sure that he did not end up "taking someone out for being a jerk." He ignored her repeated questioning about whether he "really meant that" and refused to talk about it. Below, I talk about the most common situations that new combat veterans sometimes find uncomfortable and their responses to them.

Hypervigilance

As a part of training and during deployment, service members learn to be highly aware of their surroundings and look for potential threats more or less constantly. Although being highly aware of one's surroundings is important in some situations (for example, in public, in a new situation), it may appear that your partner is often taking this approach to an extreme in a behavior termed *hypervigilance*. This may show itself in behaviors such as frequently checking locks at home or looking out of the window. Another common example might be your partner insisting to sit far away from a large plate glass window in the front of a restaurant, with his back to the wall at the rear of the establishment, near the kitchen and back exit. Or, your partner may be overprotective of you and your children, which may mean your partner objects to you traveling to a place that you would judge as safe. Hypervigilance may or may not mean your partner is experiencing post-traumatic distress disorder (PTSD)—either way, it could still affect your relationship and his ability to work through reintegration with you and your family.

Many recent service members and veterans who were deployed for combat in urban environments face criticism from others about their driving. Situations involving being blocked in traffic, approaching intersections, and the closeness of other vehicles have become associated with various threats as a result of these urban deployments. These threats include concerns of other vehicles being used as weapons, the presence of improvised explosive devices (IEDs), and being trapped in traffic and being a "sitting duck" for an attack. If this is true for your partner, this may have led to aggressive driving, including going through stoplights, going around vehicles that slow down, speeding past fuel-tanker trucks, and other risky driving behaviors. Service members and veterans who have been deployed are often reluctant to give up control of the wheel to their partners or anyone else.

The Impact on Your Relationship

These ways of thinking and behaving can have a direct impact on your relationship. You may find yourself walking on eggshells or worried that your partner will be irritable with you or will fly off the handle at your children. Your worry and attentiveness may feel to your partner as though you are watching him at all times or that you are hovering. To your partner, it may feel as if you are trying to control or intervene in every situation in the household. Despite your best intentions, it is often communicated as a lack of trust. To a service member who had the weight of a mission and important deployment responsibilities, this may feel insulting. The differences between how you view your partner and your partner's experience may feel like a wedge is being driven between the two of you.

Most military service members and veterans are highly aware of negative stereotypes about PTSD that are applied to them following military deployments, especially combat deployments. There is a stigma associated with military deployment and PTSD in the US culture, and any time your partner has a reaction that seems out of place or extreme in civilian life, he may worry that others believe something is wrong with him. Part of your partner denying having any emotional reactions that are out of his control is the desire to avoid having this stigma applied to him.

As stated above, your partner's hypervigilance about harm to you or your children may result in your partner objecting to you being in places that feel unsafe to him. This may feel as if your partner is trying to control you since you have a different idea about what is safe. This may lead to arguments about your coming and going from the house, what places are safe, and what is a reasonable risk. By questioning your partner's judgment about what is safe or not, you may imply, without realizing it, that your partner is overreacting. Your partner may then respond defensively because of the worry that this plays into the stereotype of the military service member or veteran.

In general, many intimate partners have disagreements about driving style even without deployment experiences. Spouses often believe that their partner's driving style is not very safe; these disputes are rarely resolved by each partner attempting to convince the other of the correctness of his or her driving approach. Furthermore, the veterans I have worked with who experienced some type of urban deployment are usually very confident of their skills because they have been tested in the worst possible driving conditions and survived. It may seem reasonable to try to convince your partner that his driving is not safe, but this approach will rarely lead to your partner agreeing with your argument and changing his driving habits.

Ways to Cope with Your Worry About Your Partner's Behavior

You can use several methods to turn your watching and worrying about your partner's reactions into something more positive for you both. One of the best ways is to focus first on things you like about your partner's actions, essentially balancing your view of your partner with a reminder of the things that are going well. This may feel difficult at first, especially if you believe that some of the ways your partner is reacting to deployment are affecting your children. Having a balanced view, however, will help your partner respond better to your concerns. I will also discuss how you can talk with your partner about your concerns in ways that are most likely to be successful. Much of this can be done without asking directly for any specific change from your partner but that could lead to change nonetheless. As stated above, even though your partner may not always seem willing to work in a cooperative way with you, positive changes you make will have a positive impact on your partner. Although this is hard to believe at first, it is really the only effective way of encouraging your partner to make changes that benefit you and your relationship.

Notice Positive Relationship Events

This simple procedure is highly powerful: pay attention to things that your partner does, and then say something positive to your partner about one of these behaviors at least once a day. This method is a variant of one used for clients just starting out in couples and family therapy (Falloon, Boyd, and McGill 1984; Sayers and Heyman 2002), but it can be helpful for nearly every couple because it can lead to so many types of positive changes. In fact, it is the most direct and effective method of any that I teach when working with veteran, military, and civilian couples. Why is this true? First, actively noticing positive behavior on the part of your partner changes your perspective. You stop focusing only on things you are upset about, and you feel better because you can start to see your partner's positive contributions to the relationship. Second, when you notice positive things your partner does, you are actually encouraging your partner to do them more often. Third, your partner will notice more of the positive things that you do, mostly because you have set the right tone and example for this. Last, you and your partner often become more willing to do things for the other when you have a daily focus on positive actions taken by the other.

How you carry this out, however, makes all the difference in the world. Here are the guidelines and the rationale behind each.

Look for a Specific Action or Behavior by Your Partner That You Like

The goal is to become more aware of the positive things your partner does than the things that are upsetting. This method is *opportunistic* in that you sometimes have to pay close attention and wait to see positive actions that you can comment on. This is harder than it may appear, especially when you are often upset or worried about your partner. Your partner does many things during the day, however, that you have come to take for granted or that are overshadowed in your own mind by some of the more worrisome things that he or she does.

Focusing more on negative things is a frequent error we all make, so why do humans do it? We can guess that it has something to do with attention to negative events as being useful for our survival instinct. We are programmed to perceive threat as a way to stay alive, and many believe that this extends to minor actions of others that are psychological in nature. So, as I discussed above regarding hypervigilance, we become highly attuned to things that our partner does that lead us to feel sad or hurt, such as being irritable, and we pay less attention to things our partners do that we like, such as being kind and open.

It is important to focus on an exact action or actions, such as "playing on the floor with our son," rather than broad traits, such as "being a good father." Naming specific actions makes it clearer to you and your partner which ones you value. Although a broader description such as "being a good father" may get at the heart of what it is you want from your partner, each person differs on what that means, so specifics are key. The action or behavior you focus on for any particular day should be meaningful to you but also can be a small gesture, such as making a cup of coffee for you, picking up after the kids, or some other simple task. The behavior also should be thought of as something you want to happen more and not something you want to *stop* happening.

Tell Your Partner What Actions You Are Appreciating and Make a Record for Yourself

Once a day, tell your partner in a clear and deliberate manner, the specific positive action or behavior that you appreciate and why. Be sure to mention why the action is meaningful or helpful to you personally or for the family. Say, "I really enjoyed watching you play with the kids today," or "I noticed when you were playing with the kids that I really felt great about our family."

When the behavior is more mundane, yet still meaningful, the comment could be stated this way: "I appreciate your bringing the checkbook to me for the bills; it was just a nice thing since I feel so busy much of the time." Other effective types of statements can be briefer, such as, "I liked that you called me at work today; it's nice to have that break." You can also state that the action was helpful to the two of you as a couple in the following way: "Thanks for taking the car in for service today—we never have to worry about our cars since you are always up on that."

Make sure you have your partner's attention. When you can, make eye contact, touch your partner lightly on the arm, or do something else to set the comment aside from other conversation. You may already have the type of relationship in which you commonly thank your partner in a socially appropriate way. For the purposes of highlighting the comment and having the most impact, be sure to include more detail about why the action was helpful or appreciated by you. Below are some written examples of the specific behaviors along with brief statements about these actions.

Your partner's behavior: *Bob woke the kids up this morning.*

Your statement: I appreciate that you woke the kids up today, since I think they really appreciate seeing you first thing in the morning.

Your partner's behavior: *Linda sat with me, opened the bills, and discussed them while we wrote them out.*

Your statement: Thanks for working with me on the bills. I always feel we are on the same team when we work like that.

Your partner's behavior: *Susan stood beside me and watched while I sent Sean to time-out when he threw his toy.*

Your statement: I liked when you were there just watching when I was disciplining Sean; I felt really trusted by you because I think he knew you backed me, even without saying anything. It feels like we are a team.

Your partner's behavior: *Will told me he was having pain, really distracted by Iraq stuff, and needed to lie down.*

Your statement: I think it was helpful when you let me know you were dealing with pain and memories of your deployment. Even though I couldn't do anything to help except give you some space, when you let me know what's going on I feel like I am helping in some way.

Note that some of the comments refer to everyday, mundane events, like paying the bills. Others deal directly with how you would communicate to your partner about your role in helping him cope with postdeployment struggles with physical pain or combat-related memories. The benefit of taking this approach is that you comment on behaviors that already occur but that occur less often than you prefer. If stated in a skillful way, your comment on a particular behavior makes it more likely that your partner will take this action in the future.

It is best to make written notes, using the format presented above, of both what your partner's actions were and your verbal statements. Keep these to yourself since this written record is meant only to remind you to do this at least once a day.

Trust the Power of Your Own Appreciation and Exercise Patience

One of the cornerstones of all intimate relationships is each person's ability to make his or her partner happy. Take a moment and rate, from one (least) to ten (most), *how much your partner cares and values* whether he makes you happy and feels good when he has done something that you are pleased with. Keep the rating firmly in your mind. Now, whatever your rating is, your partner's real internal feeling of pleasure when you are happy with him is probably much higher. Most of us underestimate the pleasure our partner gets when we are pleased with him or her.

Think of this in reverse—you like it when your partner sees what you do for the relationship, laughs at your jokes, and appreciates your point of view. You do not enjoy feeling taken for granted, and you like it when your partner notices your efforts around the house, when you give your partner the benefit of the doubt when something goes wrong (such as a bill not getting paid), and when you show any extra bit of kindness. Most of us are wired to enjoy making our partners happy in a wide variety of ways.

This discussion also highlights that through taking this positive approach, changes in your relationship will happen slowly. The primary reason is that each partner looks for consistency and patterns over time in order to see how things will go. If your partner is taking a wait-and-see attitude about the whole reintegration process after returning from deployment, he is likely waiting to see whether your appreciation is short lived. Also, it could be that your partner is highly distracted by figuring out his next career or educational move, and it may take repetition of your commenting on positive events in your relationship over days and weeks to be noticed. Be prepared to try this method out for at least two weeks before expecting any increase in how positive things are in your relationship or any verbal reaction on the part of your partner to your comments.

Keep the Statements Positive

Make your statements about your partner's behavior totally positive and avoid any hint of negativity. It is not useful to "score points" against your partner, and any negative part of the statement will almost eliminate the value of it to your partner. There are many ways a statement can be made negative, but presented below are some common things to avoid and some alternatives.

- Avoid talking about the past: "I love it when you play with the kids; they really noticed when you stayed away from them when you first got back." Alternative: "I love it when you play with the kids; they really like it when you do things with them."

- Avoid mentioning your unhappiness when your partner fails to perform the action: "I'm glad you paid that bill because every time you miss it, our credit score gets worse and worse." Alternative: "I'm glad you paid that bill because it helps our credit score go in the right direction."

- Avoid implying that an action rarely or never happens: "Thanks for bringing the cup of coffee. You hardly ever do that anymore." Alternative: "Thanks for the cup of coffee. I always love it when you bring one to me."

Each of the alternatives presented above removes the implied barb in the second half of the statement and implies that your relationship and family are going in the right direction.

Potential Negative Reactions and Concerns

Your partner may have one or more negative reactions to your comments, perhaps by being defensive or suspicious. If you sound as if you are making too much of any particular action, it may come across to your partner as you looking down on him or acting like a parent with him. You will know that this has happened if your partner responds defensively to a comment about a kind behavior, saying, for example, "Of course I do nice things for you—when did you start seeing me as not nice?" It will help if you use your usual, normal manner of speaking when recognizing a contribution by your partner. Trust that simply noticing an action by your partner and mentioning it are very powerful. Your best verbal response to defuse a defensive reaction might be to say, "I probably got that across to you wrong—I just want you to know that I noticed, and I liked it. I think I should be telling you when I appreciate something you've done." Remember that appreciation between you and your partner can and should be an exchange between equals. Your partner likely has his own standards for how to behave as a partner and parent. It is important that you make it clear that you are letting your partner know how you personally feel and are not trying to set a standard for correct behavior as a partner or parent.

You may also receive suspiciousness from your partner with this type of response: "What are you up to with always commenting on what I do?" Your response can be similar to the one just described, namely, "I really don't mean anything by it. I just want you to know that I noticed, and I liked it. I may not be as appreciative as I really need to be." If you are guessing that your partner has become hypersensitive to your comments, take a day or so break before saying out loud the actions that you are noticing every day. In general, if you get a sense that your partner is irritated by your positive comments for one reason or another, you can always take a brief break. Make sure, however, that you are pausing because you got the sense that it was not received well, not because you are frustrated or feeling down about your progress as a couple. Feeling frustrated and down is likely a part of a downward trend as a couple; focusing on positive actions is a helpful way out of this trend that can benefit both of you.

You may be concerned that the things you do for your partner are taken for granted, so when do you get a chance to be recognized for the nice things you do? First, by taking the initiative yourself, you may prompt your partner to become more aware of positive contributions by both of you in the relationship. Second, one of the things you can comment on are the instances in which your partner notices and comments on your own behavior. You can encourage your partner to make these kinds of comments also. This may sound complicated at first, but it is really straightforward. Here is an example: "*Thanks for noticing* that I cleaned out the car; I'm trying to do things that help both of us, and *I like it when you let me know I'm focusing on the right thing*." The words in italics indicate the parts of the statement that refer to your partner's noticing your positive contributions and telling you about it.

Discussing Your Concerns with Your Partner

Once you have focused on the positive things that your partner is doing using the methods discussed above, you have increased the chances that your partner will react well when you talk directly about the behaviors you are worried about. It is important to remember that whatever the challenges you are feeling with your partner's reintegration into your relationship, this is only a part of the larger challenge your partner feels in adjusting to life after deployment since he may also be making big life decisions about education or a new career. There are several approaches discussed below that will convey respect about that challenge and that your partner is ultimately responsible for the choices he needs to make. These approaches include

- opening up the lines of communication,

- validating your partner's experience, and

- giving feedback.

Opening Up the Lines of Communication

This is the perfect opportunity for you to use some of the methods discussed earlier in the section on increasing intimacy (chapter 3). Asking your partner to talk to you about what he is experiencing is essentially making a bid for intimacy, with the focus on your partner sharing his personal feelings. For example, when your partner blows up at you and says, "Why didn't you tell me you were headed down into the city this afternoon?" instead of defending your reasons, pause and say gently, "Hmm. Hey, tell me what's up? I can't tell what you are responding to." This takes some practice, mostly in making yourself pause and not responding defensively and with exasperation. One tip: concentrate on the question in your mind about what is occurring in your partner's experience that leads him to talk that way. This will help lead you away from other thoughts about how unreasonable or controlling your partner is acting. If your partner is unwilling to say, you might approach him later and say, "Before, when you asked me about going down into the city, I was surprised at how worried you seemed. Can you tell me about what your concern was?"

Validate Your Partner Even When You Object to Your Partner's Reactions

You can help your partner come to terms with some of the behaviors you are worried about by *validating* and discussing your partner's experiences with him. This does not mean you like what you are seeing or that you do not have a valid concern about the impact on your family. What it does mean is that you are aware of what your partner has gone through as a service member and that the impact of these training and deployment experiences on his current behavior is common and understandable. Validating your partner's experiences will provide a better basis for expressing concern about these behaviors and how you might support your partner in adjusting to life after deployment.

You can validate your partner's experiences by commenting when you observe that your partner is having a difficult time that may be related to his deployment. For example, your partner may push back angrily when you say that your family is hosting a Fourth of July cookout and that they want you and your partner to attend. Although you do not want to miss another family event, you can validate your partner by saying, "I know you hate those big family parties, especially with the fireworks bringing everything back. I do realize that's not the kind of thing you like to be around."

If your partner responds to your request to describe a reaction to something, remember that you can encourage your partner to talk more freely by summarizing briefly what he says and by asking for more information. For example, if your partner says, "I told you before that you should wait until I'm with you before you go into the city," you can respond, "Okay, so your concern is that something will happen to me if you are not there. Can you say more about what you are concerned about?"

Give Feedback to Your Partner

When your partner has reacted to a threat that you do not see or has responded with greater forcefulness or anger than you feel is helpful or appropriate, you probably will want to let your partner know how you view the situation. Your feedback can be very useful as an alternative viewpoint. But, make sure your expectations are modest, especially for your partner's immediate reaction. Providing an alternative view of a situation may be difficult for your partner to accept if your partner believes that quick reactions, targeted aggression when needed, and a well-trained ability to detect threats kept him alive during a combat deployment. It will probably take some time and later reflection for your partner to be able to consider an alternative viewpoint.

Here are several points to keep in mind when preparing to discuss your concerns with your partner:

- It is normal and common for you and your partner to have a different way of looking at a situation or to want a different solution to a problem; differences in viewpoints are common for all couples.

- Your partner may often feel that his reaction to a situation has nothing directly to do with the military deployment but instead is due to more common hassles such as chronic pain, lack of sleep, and general frustration.

- Your feedback should be phrased as *information* for your partner, not as scolding him.

- It is important to remain interested in what your partner is experiencing and why; try not to dismiss your partner's viewpoint since that will be felt by your partner as a lack of respect.

- Your partner may find it painful (embarrassing, shameful, humiliating) to talk about how his deployment is affecting him now.

- Try to seek a compromise or a middle-ground solution to situations in which your partner sees a threat that you do not or reacts with stronger anger than is comfortable for you.

Putting all of the guidelines together in one or two statements requires some practice. It will be helpful if you try writing out your response briefly for situations that occur frequently. This is not so you have a script to read to your partner when something happens but so you have a calm, respectful way of communicating your point of view. Below are several examples of feedback based on common situations for veterans and their partners. Although these examples appear as short paragraphs, you are more likely to get these points across in a back-and-forth dialogue with your partner:

- "I was surprised when you raised your voice at Cameron for spilling his cereal, but maybe there was something going on at that moment for you. That seemed louder and tougher than he needed at this point, and it was upsetting to me, so maybe at some point we can talk about different ways to approach it."

- "I get kind of concerned when I realize I haven't seen you in the house for a while, and you're playing video games in the basement; there's a lot going on with the kids, all while I'm trying to get dinner on the table. It's frustrating for me at that time, but I realize there might be something going on that makes it difficult for you to be around all that chaos—can you tell me what's up?"

- "I know it is tough for you to plan going out to a movie, since I know you're not yet all that comfortable with it. Personally I consider it a fairly safe situation, although I realize you see more risks than I do. Still, I would like to figure out a way we can compromise on the time of day we go or type of movie we see that will make it possible for us to do that again."

Feedback About Risky Driving

As noted before, talking about driving for many couples is a challenge that probably did not start with a military deployment. Most couples have a long history of good-natured kidding or even major disputes about driving. There are a few important points about giving feedback about driving to your partner when you feel that his driving is uncomfortable or dangerous for you.

First, avoid debating the objective safety of your partner's driving. This is an argument that no one will win. What feels safe to the driver, who is controlling the vehicle, feels very different from the passenger's standpoint. It is best that anything you say about your partner's driving be based on your discomfort, which is something your partner cannot argue about. Incidentally, your partner's driving is also based on his feeling of discomfort with the aspects of the traffic and reminders of roadside threats learned through training or deployment. If you have respect for your partner's discomfort while driving, it is more likely your partner will have respect for your discomfort, and some compromise can eventually be reached. For example, you might state the following: "When we are driving on the highway I get pretty tense, although I understand you are also pretty uncomfortable."

Be reasonable and clear with yourself what your goals are in giving your partner feedback. By telling your partner about your anxiety or fear when he is driving, you are providing information that you want your partner to take into account. A reasonable goal for your feedback might be your partner's modifying some aspects of driving, although this may take some time and patience on your part. It is not likely that your partner will quickly alter his driving style despite how nice or reasonable your request is. To express these sentiments, you can say, "I know that you're pretty tense when we drive, and then I get tense with your driving; I hope over time we can work out a way we can do this so that we're not both a jumble of nerves and jumping down each other's throats."

Be specific about the aspects of driving that are of most concern to you. For example, for some recent veterans, the most obvious threat they perceive while driving might be fuel-tanker trucks, so they may speed quickly past them to put the threat behind them. If this is the driving behavior that concerns you the most, you might say, "When you speed past the tanker trucks, I understand that you're getting away from them because of the risk you see, but it really scares me. I am hoping there's another way to deal with the tankers that will feel different to me."

Make sure that you let your partner know when you become more comfortable with his driving, but in this case you might be less specific about why. The rationale behind being less specific in saying how your partner is driving differently is that it helps your partner feel less like you are directly controlling his driving (less like your complaints made him change driving habits). For example, you can say, "It seems like driving is going better for both of us. I am much more comfortable when we drive together." Your partner may attribute your increased comfort with trusting him more or simply getting used to the driving; you might consider this an acceptable outcome, especially if the overall goal is your increased sense of comfort and safety with your partner's driving.

Final Words

After deployment, your partner may communicate less and seem to withhold important information about feelings, decisions, and future plans. In addition, you might notice greater expressions of anger; at the same time, your partner might describe a lack of emotion. In addition, your partner may have an increased sense of hypervigilance about threats you do not see. These ways of thinking and behaving are common and expected reactions to military training and deployment experiences. Although these tendencies will likely decrease naturally over time, you can work with your partner to limit the negative impact on your relationship.

You can balance your concern about how your partner is acting by carefully focusing on your partner's positive behavior in your relationship. By making sure your comments about what you see are purely positive, regular, and consistent over time, you can help both you and your partner become more aware of each other's contributions to the relationship. Attention to behavior can be motivating for your partner because each of you feels better when you know that you have the ability to please, support, and delight your partner.

Feedback to your partner who displays irritability, hypervigilance, or withdrawn behavior can be helpful as long as it is not overly negative and shows respect for your partner's internal worries and fears. It often takes several invitations for your partner to freely discuss these feelings with you. At the same time, you can communicate how these behaviors lead to unhappiness for you, but it helps to demonstrate the willingness to listen to your partner's perspective and to compromise on any situation. You can even give your partner feedback about risky driving, but remember that these approaches take time and patience.

Chapter 6

Making It Work

"We just decided a long time ago that it didn't matter what happened; we were not going to split—we were going to find a way to make things work."

—*Charlene*

As part of a couple reintegrating after a military deployment, you face more than the usual number of challenges couples typically do. This can be a time of upheaval, including transition from military to civilian life, relocation, helping your partner deal with minor or major chronic physical or emotional injuries, and you or your partner launching into school or a new career. You may also have young children to consider, and their care continues to be a daily need. But there are several things discussed in this chapter that are under your control and that will help you, your partner, and your family adjust well. In addition, this chapter will focus on putting together the skills discussed so far in a long-term strategy for helping your relationship change and prosper.

Keys to Success in Reintegration

There are many factors in successful reintegration, so I hesitate to boil them down to a few major suggestions. Fortunately, clinical experiences and research over the past several decades have identified a few aspects of relationships that are under your control that can determine how well you and your partner recover from conflict and have more lasting success at working together. Some of the factors discussed below underline those discussed earlier in this book, such as how beliefs and ways of thinking can have an impact on your feelings and behavior.

Relationship Commitment

When working with couples who have gone through reintegration after a military deployment, I have frequently been impressed by the power of the partners' commitment to one another. The couples who handled all the challenges in this period well made a decision that they would not consider divorce for almost any reason. These partners made a firm commitment to put great effort and patience toward resolving the problems that they might face before leaving the relationship. One former marine stated it humorously this way: "She told me under no circumstances was she going to ever go to the trouble of looking for somebody else, so I guess we're in it for the long haul. Neither of us are going anywhere." Although he downplayed his role in the acceptance of this commitment, the rest of the conversation revealed a deep promise to resolving the issues they faced, tolerating their differences, and staying together their entire lives.

Recent research supports that true commitment to the relationship is associated with greater happiness in couples (Rhoades, Stanley, and Markman 2010). True commitment involves a sense of dedication, of making a clear and conscious decision that you will work hard to stay in the relationship. There are other sources of commitment that may lead people to decide to stay in a relationship. These sources of commitment work more like *constraints*, or factors that prevent people from leaving relationships. Examples are material things (Rhoades, Stanley, and Markman 2010), such as joint ownership of pets and having a lease or mortgage together. Other sources include feeling trapped and social pressure to stay together by friends and family members. Generally, couples who have commitment associated with dedication, material constraints, and difficulties associated with separating tend to stay together; those who feel only trapped, however, are more likely to separate and divorce (Rhoades, Stanley, and Markman 2010).

Being dedicated and committed to your partner appears to be the best way you can stay together and help ensure that you are happy. Why would this be the case? Intimate relationships typically begin with a great deal of love and excitement. As your lives became intertwined, children entered into the picture, work lives got busier, and day-to-day stress might have stretched your ability to work well as a team. Adding in the changes brought to your relationship by a military deployment, the pressures you face have risen. Only those dedicated to continuing to work better as a couple and to building new skills will thrive in their relationship.

For example, William and Collette were struggling two years after Collette had been deployed to Afghanistan as a medic. It was her second wartime deployment, and one year ago they had decided that it was time for Collette to leave the army to get pregnant. After a year of trying to conceive, they realized it was not going well, and they were faced with the possibility of expensive medical treatment. The couple often argued about how they would afford this, since William was in school using his own GI benefits to finish his undergraduate degree. Furthermore, the partners rarely had sex except to try to get pregnant. Understanding that they faced several important decisions, William and Collette began to devote a brief time each week to go through their options. They started with talking about what was most important to them: each other, having children, and financial stability. After recognizing that they still shared the same values, they recommitted to reaching their goals by working together. They agreed to reconsider all of their short-term work and educational plans and explored all the different possible ways of developing a family without risking their financial situation. The primary ingredient in their success at working together was committing to each other as a team.

Setting Aside Anger and Hopelessness and Encouraging Change

When I talk to couples who are unhappy, each partner nearly always has valid complaints against the other. Furthermore, among military and veteran couples who have sacrificed a great deal as a couple, there is plenty for both partners to feel angry about when the couple is stressed. But we each have the ability to let our anger become destructive, leading us to say or do hurtful things. After months and years of these feelings, you may feel worn down and hopeless about how things can improve. You desperately want to make your partner change some things about how she is treating you. What should be done with all these feelings? Although these feelings occur naturally, they prevent you from making progress in reintegration. We all have ways of helping maintain these types of feelings and have to make an effort to reduce the negative influence of emotions that get in our way.

Letting Go of Angry Thoughts

It is important to decide to let go of anger. We each have this ability but often choose not to use it because we assume that we have a justifiable reason to be angry. But, it is not necessary to be extremely angry in order to decide to seek a change in how you and your partner relate to one another. Actually, continuing to have a high level of anger can prevent you from solving problems effectively with your partner.

Consider Carol and Adam's current stalemate. Since the return from his last deployment in Afghanistan, Adam has not been able to sleep very well. He spends a good deal of time at home playing the *Call of Duty* video game, which helps distract him from all the chaos going on in the house with his young kids. Carol expects him to help more, to talk to her more about what is going on with him, and to go out with her from time to time. She has been angry for months about Adam's disappearing to play the game and not helping out even though he keeps promising to do more. He is tired of her not seeing all that he does around the house, and feels she just yells at him any time they talk. Carol feels that she is justified at being angry at Adam and that she needs to be on his case or else he will think he is doing fine. From her point of view, not being angry will just signal that he is right and she is wrong. Her anger, however, leads her to speak sharply to Adam much of the time and to sound harsh and difficult. She does not see that she has some choices in how to approach this problem.

Feeling righteous anger, as justified as it may be, may not actually help you improve your relationship since it may get in the way. You can identify the thoughts that generate and nurture your anger and replace them with thoughts that generate less anger. You can use the list below to think about what you feel angry about and check off the thoughts that are similar to yours.

Common Anger Thoughts

- *She shouldn't treat me this way.*

- *He is trying to get back at me for not going along with what he wants.*

- *I deserve more respect for all I did to keep the house and the family together while she was away.*

- *I will not stand for this type of treatment—I have my own needs.*

- *He is being unreasonable and never compromises.*

- *She always gets what she wants—I never do.*

These thoughts might feel true and correct for you, but they suffer from several common problems. Some of these thoughts are expressed in terms of black and white. The words *never* and *always* are not likely to be factually correct since there are often exceptions. Like the phrase "I will not stand for...," these thoughts tend to lead you to be unbending in your approach rather than to continue to look for solutions that work for both of you. Drawing a line in the sand may work for enemies but rarely works well with the people we love. Several of the thoughts imply *blame* in that they do not take your partner's viewpoint into account. They imply negative motives in your partner ("My partner is trying to get back at me"), which may be untrue, or negative traits ("My partner is unreasonable and never compromises"), which amount to name calling. The secret to feeling less angry is coming up with ways of thinking about your partner and your concerns that feel true but serve you better.

More useful thoughts are often more complex, more specific, and require a little more work.

Useful Replacements for Angry Thoughts

- *My partner often sounds so harsh with me—I will continue to stick up for myself and let her know I am not happy about being spoken to this way.*

- *He may be acting in anger toward me—I need to encourage him to talk to me about what is going on since I assume he's just as angry as I am about how things are going.*

- *I know the deployment was hard for my partner, but I worked hard too. I need to keep insisting that she talk to me with a respectful tone.*

- *I am not happy with the current situation; we both have needs that we have to juggle in this relationship.*

- *He has taken a hard-line approach to this issue, and I need to encourage us both to be in a more compromising frame of mind.*

- *She is often focused on winning an argument. Both of us feel like we are losing out.*

More useful and accurate thoughts tend to be more even-handed. They express things that your partner faces and are focused on the best way to combat the problem. You do not need to give in on what you feel is important about the situation. Being less angry and more focused on the solution will give you more energy to devote to encouraging your partner to work cooperatively with you. You can use the following format for this exercise.

Angry thought: My partner is trying to get back at me.

Replacement thought: My partner strikes back when upset at things I've said. We need to take a calmer approach rather than just criticizing each other so much.

Angry thought: _____

_____

Replacement thought: _____

_____

Alternatives to Hopelessness

Unsatisfying relationships are similar to clinical depression in several ways (Epstein 1985). People who are depressed feel that they have few positive experiences and view the world (including relationships) in mostly negative ways; partners in a relationship that is working poorly have this same feeling. In both depression and unhappy relationships, people tend to look for bad things to happen, perhaps to confirm their expectations that things will not go well. We all have hopeless thoughts from time to time, but this is only a problem when these feelings are consistent over time.

If you are feeling hopeless because of your situation, then you may believe that you are simply reacting to the reality of the situation. But carrying this feeling prevents you from making the best decision and reduces the amount of energy you have to deal with your struggles. For example, in the scenario described with Carol and Adam above, Carol felt hopeless about Adam's playing video games since it had gone on for months. Unfortunately, her belief that this problem was unsolvable made it difficult for her to work with Adam to solve it and actually fueled her hopelessness.

Below are the types of thoughts that tend to maintain hopelessness about the problems you may face with the reintegration of your own partner after deployment. Do you have any of these thoughts on a consistent basis?

Common Hopelessness Thoughts

- *Things will never get better.*

- *Am I just going to have to deal with fights about his reactions to the kids until they are grown?*

- *The war changed my partner in ways we can't control.*

- *I can't keep fighting with my partner this way.*

- *We never have any fun together anymore.*

- *We have an endless series of problems, one after another.*

The problem with hopeless thoughts are that they are vague and they highlight the aspects of the problems that are not under your control. The goals in finding more hopeful ways of thinking are finding positive exceptions and finding the parts of the problem that are under your control. Listed below are some alternative ways of thinking that challenge hopelessness.

Alternatives to Hopelessness Thoughts

- *Things have been tough for a while, but that doesn't mean that we have to keep doing the same things and feeling bad about it.*

- *My partner is struggling with her reactions to the kids right now. Each age is going to bring some challenges, and we need to keep looking for ways to work better as a family.*

- *The war was a big challenge for my partner and our family, but we have choices about how we respond to these challenges.*

- *We've been arguing this way for a while; it's time to try some new approaches to our problems.*

- *We have not been having fun as a couple or a family. I am going to place more priority on things we enjoy.*

In each case, alternative thoughts that combat hopelessness focus on making new choices and the possibility of change. These thoughts, however, do not sugarcoat the current situation. Instead, they acknowledge that things are not going positively. Combating hopelessness, then, does not involve being unrealistic. Changing hopeless thoughts also takes some effort and practice. It requires a more balanced and disciplined approach to interpreting your situation. Try writing down some of your hopeless thoughts, and then come up with some realistic alternatives. It is important to write these thoughts down on paper, since it is easier to produce alternatives in a more objective way when you are looking at the thoughts in front of you. As you work on this task, note that your thoughts about the task itself may be hopeless thoughts (for example, *This writing exercise won't help at all*). You may want to include these thoughts on your list also, followed by more realistic and forward-looking thoughts that combat the feeling of hopelessness. You can use the format described above for writing about changing angry thoughts.

Encouraging Change with an Uncooperative Partner

You may have a feeling that your partner is not working with you to adjust to changes in your partner's return to the family after a deployment. For example, Felicia had been trying to get Thomas, an Army National Guard member who had deployed to Afghanistan, to spend more time with her socializing with their old friends. He told her that their old friends did not "get what it was like" during the deployment, and he did not want to educate them. She also was concerned about some of their bills since she had seen a couple of late notices in the mail, but every time Felicia brought it up, he told her he was handling it. He spent more and more time in his workshop although she was not sure he was doing much there. Felicia's biggest concern was that she did not understand why Thomas was not being cooperative and open in response to her attempts to work with him to have more enjoyment and to handle the bills in a better way.

What accounts for your own partner's lack of cooperation? There are several possibilities. Your partner may be reacting to feeling pressured or forced when you are talking to her about a particular problem. As described in chapter 4, when people feel like their choices are narrowed, it affects their need for autonomy, or the drive to make decisions and choices without being forced by others. Second, the overall task of reintegration for your partner may be overwhelming; she may be avoiding dealing with you directly about family issues. Many service members who enter civilian life report that life outside the mission of a deployment is much more complicated than the deployment, which was hard but clear and defined. This can lead your partner to set aside issues that are less clear and require a great deal of discussion. Even if your partner is not overwhelmed, her focus might be on entering a new career, starting school, getting service benefits from the US Department of Veterans Affairs (VA), all while dealing with chronic pain from service-related injuries. Third, emotional burdens, including anxiety, depression, or guilt related to deployment, may make it difficult for your partner to work with you fully on adjusting within your family or in new activities outside the family. Your partner may also be dealing with several of the above problems at once.

There are several ways to help your partner be more cooperative with your attempts to improve your relationship and the adjustment to reintegration. Start by trying to open up lines of communication with your partner to learn which of these issues, if any, she is struggling with. This may help you find some solutions for working better with your partner, such as knowing when is a good time to talk versus when your partner needs time to rest due to pain or feeling overwhelmed. Methods of inviting your partner to talk to you about problems such as these are discussed in chapter 3.

If your partner is feeling pressured by you, at times you will need to step back from trying to change how your partner is dealing with you or your children. It is important to understand that many of the changes you want your partner to make are increases in actions or behaviors that your partner does infrequently rather than not at all. The absolute best approach is to use the method described in chapter 5, to focus on your partner's positive behavior and let her know that you are pleased about seeing it when it occurs. In fact, most of the positive changes you want from your partner can be achieved by following and commenting on things you want your partner to do more often. This will be discussed more in the next section.

Now that I have described many of the methods that you can use to deal with reintegration problems, in the next section I will present the strategy of putting them together.

Putting It All Together

I have described several specific skills for dealing with the types of reintegration issues you may experience. Each of these skills has a place, but it will be helpful to have an overall strategy for thinking about them and taking action. For instance, when do you focus on your partner's behavior, when do you ask your partner to come up with solutions to a particular problem, and when do you just share your feelings about an issue, with no clear goal to solve it? There are several guidelines for knowing *what* to do and *when.*

Methods for Using Your Relationship Skills

The general rule for approaching change and improvements in how you and your partner deal with deployment reintegration challenges involves two factors: (1) positive day-to-day experiences with your partner should far outweigh the negative experiences, and (2) less focus should be placed on direct changes of your partner and more should be placed on changes in your own behavior and your approach to your relationship's challenges. The first factor is clear; you and your partner benefit most by having the most positive experiences possible when you are adjusting to her return. The second factor recognizes that you only have direct control over yourself; and, as I have covered in previous chapters, you can actually have tremendous impact on your partner with changes you make in your own approach. Therefore, prioritize the methods below in the order they are presented. Positive experiences are the most important and are where you should put most of your efforts. Also note that while it is important to be able to resolve conflict and tension, if you spend most of your efforts resolving conflict, you and your partner will feel drained by your relationship.

Build Positive Experiences First

The most important goal is to make sure your day-to-day and weekly time spent with your partner are as positive as possible. This is where your skills for sharing thoughts and feelings and scheduling time to do enjoyable activities with your partner become important. Researchers of close relationships have described positive time with one's partner as depositing money in a bank account of positive emotion (Gottman 2011). When you have an argument, you are spending resources from this bank account. The higher the balance on the account, the safer your relationship is. Not only do these positive times together help insulate you from tougher times, you and your partner deserve to enjoy each other—especially given your sacrifices.

Although previous chapters have presented some examples of ways to spend enjoyable time together, below is a short list of simple things you can do that cost little or no money.

Ideas for Simple and Fun Things to Do

- Share a cup of morning coffee on the porch or patio while reading the paper.
- Go for a walk or bike ride around the block or neighborhood.
- Listen to music.
- Go out to brunch at a diner.

- Exercise together.
- Read the same book.

Making this time with your partner enjoyable involves some discipline and focus to ensure that talk of unpleasant topics and household tasks does not get in the way. These topics not only take up time from enjoying your partner, they tend to cast a shadow over the time you have set aside to enjoy one another's company. You can suggest to your partner that the issue can be dealt with at your weekly meeting or some other time when business is conducted. If you are often in the role of bringing up relationship or family issues to your partner that need to be addressed, she will appreciate that you are able to actively set these problems aside for the sake of enjoyment.

Slow Down and Try to Change One Thing at a Time

Trying to limit your attempts to change things in the way you and your partner are adjusting in the reintegration period after a deployment might sound opposite of your overall goal. You will find, however, that the more you push for changes, the fewer changes will occur. It is best to decide which changes should happen first and which can wait. For example, Bill wanted Sharon, who had returned from deployment to Kuwait two years ago, to spend more time at home during the weekends with him and their kids, to be more open to him sexually, and to go over their financial plan for the future. Sharon often responded angrily when he brought these issues up, saying she was already overburdened with school and work and he would just have to deal with it himself. Bill decided to focus on time with him and their kids to make sure they connected in an enjoyable way at least once a week. After talking with Sharon about this main concern, they decided to have a game night once a week, alternating the next week with movie night. And this type of success can build on itself—it does not have to be a stopping place.

Rely First on the Impact of Appreciation of Positive Behavior

As described in chapter 5, there is so much more power in your following and commenting on your partner's positive behavior than you realize, compared to complaining about your partner's negative behavior. I want to add here another reason for using this method. Focusing on positive behavior can be seen as your main method of influencing your partner's actions. It is often better than directly asking your partner to treat you and your kids differently, because it completely respects your partner's choices. Your partner can decide whether and when to act in a way that pleases you. By not asking directly, you also avoid setting up an emotional burden or expectation with your partner that clouds the positive meaning of whatever action you want from her. For example, if you say to your partner, "I really need you to start helping get the kids ready for school every morning," each time your partner does not help in the morning, then she has disappointed or angered you. Thus, she has to weigh the cost of deciding not to do what you ask (which is disappointing you) against helping with the kids and feeling hassled and impatient with them (which is a different kind of cost). Instead, when you simply notice and comment on when she does help with the kids, your partner may feel appreciated and encouraged to do this but still has the freedom to choose when to help. Also, this method is clear and aboveboard—your partner will know that when she is able to make choices that you like, you will notice and be appreciative, but when this is not possible, there is no negative emotional payback.

Use Your Own Example to Set Patterns

Another way to shift your partner's behavior is to be a good leader and to provide a clear and consistent example of what you would like to happen. The best way to do this is in the method described above, to follow and comment on your partner's positive behavior. If you and your partner are struggling as a couple, you can still set the emotional tone for the family by limiting complaints about the way things are going. Instead you can encourage any action that your partner or any family member has done by simply commenting on it. The impact of this positive approach is much greater than you think, and you are demonstrating to your partner and children an effective way of relating to each other.

Setting an example is clearly just a beginning, and if you would like some specific change, you may need to say more. Usually, if the change is something important for you, a longer discussion is necessary. For example, greeting one another when coming or leaving the house may be part of important values for you —those values being the importance of daily affection and staying emotionally connected. You can first use the skills discussed in chapter 3 about intimacy to explain your values and your feelings about why the action (daily greeting) is important. Second, you can watch for instances in which greetings occur and acknowledge nonverbally with a smile or by simply noting "Thanks, I like it when we connect regularly."

Use of Weekly Meetings and Brief, Regular Check-Ins

The skill that it is important to develop after your partner has returned from a deployment is the ability to discuss issues briefly and to effectively make decisions. For noncontroversial issues, many decisions can be made quickly after you and your partner agree that an issue is a problem that needs to be solved. You and your partner can then use brainstorming, as described in chapter 4, to generate as many solutions as possible.

If you have not been able to develop the routine of weekly meetings with your partner, then the important ideas for brief and effective meetings can still be followed. The discussion works best when it is mostly focused on the business aspects of your relationship and family, has a clear agenda so you and your partner know the goal, and stays focused on solutions to the problems at hand.

Conflict Resolution

The term *conflict resolution* covers how conflicts are managed as well as how an end to the conflict is reached. Below I expand the discussion begun in earlier chapters about communication guidelines and discuss what you and your partner might think is a good result to a fight between the two of you.

What Is Fighting Fair?

The term *fighting fair* is a little misleading—the goal is actually to make sure a disagreement, even a heated one, does not become a fight. I described in chapter 4 that blaming and name calling, as well as dwelling on the past, are things to avoid when trying to solve a problem. Here are some more guidelines to help avert a fight.

Types of Communication to Avoid

- **Putting your partner down.** This is done in many ways, including placing your partner in a bad light ("When you were yelling at me at the party, everyone thought you were losing it") and reminding her of mistakes or faults.

- **Threats.** You might threaten to leave your partner when you are angry, to take the children, or to go to his family if things do not improve.

- **Using guilt and playing the victim.** In this type of statement, you repeatedly describe to your partner how much she has purposely hurt or harmed you, without admitting any responsibility. "You have no idea what a jerk you're being to me!" This is different from stating that your partner has done something that has resulted in your feeling bad.

- **Repeating yourself.** It is easy to repeat yourself if your partner has not made it clear you have been heard. When we repeat things, we usually try to say it louder and with more force, which can lead to a more intense argument.

- **Pursuing your partner during an argument.** Following your partner if he is attempting to leave the room during the argument usually makes your partner feel trapped. Your partner is probably trying to leave because the emotions he feels are hard to tolerate without also acting angry, unpleasant, or physically violent.

For the most part, we tend to use the types of comments and tactics on the list above to strike back at our partners when we are angry and hurt. Knowing when you are most likely to say these things is the first step. The second is to choose not to say them. This requires you to be honest about your own actions, and also to see the long-term value in not harming your partner and her feelings. (The use of alcohol also tends to make it more likely that you say the types of things on the list above.)

Using Time-Outs

It is helpful to learn to take a break or time-out, by separating and then coming back together at a later time to continue the discussion more calmly. Either you or your partner can signal to the other that a break from the discussion is needed. Here is one way to do this: "I am feeling really heated; let's take a break and talk about this in about thirty minutes. Can we meet back here then?" Even if your partner is also angry, it may be best to talk about your state of mind and not your partner's. The suggestion ends in a question so that your partner's choice in the matter is clear.

Your partner may signal before you do that she is going to leave the argument by saying one of the following: "I'm outta here," "This is getting ridiculous, I'm not wasting my time with this discussion," or "This is going nowhere." You can still suggest a time-out by stating evenly: "You're right—we are not getting anywhere. Can we talk again in about thirty minutes (or an hour) when things are calmer? We can restart then on a better note."

During the time separated from one another, make sure you do not stew about the argument. If that is happening, pay attention to your thoughts; you are likely thinking about things said that were hurtful and how wronged you feel. It is better to distract yourself with another, more pleasant activity before turning to think about the problem. If you do spend some time thinking about the problem, try to focus on what you would like to happen and all the ways the problem might be solved. Once the agreed-upon time has elapsed, ask your partner whether she is ready to talk about the issue again briefly. If your partner says she is not ready, let the issue go for the time being, stating: "That's fine. At some point, let's talk through this to come to a decision."

Recovering from an Argument

It may be tough to come back together to discuss a problem after highly intense and hurtful arguments. Think about the last several arguments you and your partner had. How did it end? Make a note to yourself of the answers to the following questions about what usually happens.

Recovery from Arguments

- How did the main part of the argument end? (Who left the argument? Was something thrown or a wall punched?)

- Did you or your partner attempt to make up? How? Did either of you apologize or forgive the other?

- Were you, as a couple, able to make up? Did you resume arguing?

- How many hours or days were there between the start of the argument and when things were normal again?

- Were you and your partner able to discuss the problem calmly at a later time?

- Did you make progress toward a solution?

After intense arguments what is often needed is a period of time for recovery and healing. There are several parts to this, including (1) apology and forgiveness, (2) signaling a truce, and (3) team building. Not all of these are required, but the most effective recovery usually includes all three. Apologies are difficult for many people because they imply admitting fault and giving up on your position and needs. You do not have to give up what you need and want, but it is always helpful to admit when you have made some error in communicating. For example, you can state, "I am really sorry we argued; I know I said some things that made you mad, and I want to apologize." If your partner is able to provide an apology, do your best to accept it. You are not saying that what occurred was okay but simply that you accept the attempt at an apology. If your partner is only able to say, "I am sorry you were so mad at me," then accept the attempt as best you can. You can state, "I appreciate what you are trying to say because I really don't enjoy being mad at you," since this accepts your partner's best attempt to mend fences.

The second part of recovery is signaling a truce, or letting your partner know that you would like to move on and not resume the argument. There are several ways to say this, including the following: "I know it often does not go well when we try to talk about the problem with the kids; I will do my best to avoid the things that lead to an argument," or "Listen, I really don't like to argue, and I know you don't either."

The third part of recovery involves trying to get your partner to work *with* you again so that you form a team. You will need to make a verbal invitation and then make some initial suggestions about how to go about the discussion so your partner can feel reassured that it will proceed in a better way. Examples of this type of invitation include the following: "Let's try this again, but at a time when we are not tired at the end of the day. Can we set aside some time on Saturday morning to talk about it?" or "Can we try again to work this out? I think we can do better next time if we focus on this issue alone."

What Is Your Goal?

In order to avoid intense arguments for some important problems, you will need to think clearly about what you want the result to be. In some cases you may just want your partner to listen and to try to understand what you are saying. In others, you and your partner disagree about what or how something should be done, such as disciplining kids or whether you or your partner should work outside the home. Your task is always easier if you are sure that you are not asking for a specific change or to make an important decision. When your partner appears unwilling to listen to you, it is likely because she is trying to resist the feeling that you are getting the upper hand in the issue you are arguing about. If you are clear about wanting to just air your feelings about an issue, consider using the methods discussed in chapter 3 to share feelings and ideas about the problem. For example, you may be worried about how one of your children is doing in school, and you want to talk to your partner about it. You know from past arguments that you and your partner often disagree about how to deal with the kids, but in this case, you are not sure about what you think about it. You might say to your partner, "I'd like to talk about James and how things are going at school. I want to let you know what I see going on and also wanted to get your input too. Probably nothing to decide now, I just wanted to talk about it."

Of course there are times that you in fact want some type of change from your partner or need to make a decision about an important problem. This requires a more careful approach. Below I describe how to put your problem-solving skills into action for more difficult problems.

Getting to a Resolution

Make sure that you and your partner are ready to discuss the problem in a relatively calm state. This may be difficult, but there are several ways to make this more likely. First, have an initial discussion without trying to solve the problem, as described above, just to air your feelings and beliefs about the problem. This discussion should focus on fears, concerns, and values so you and your partner understand what emotions are behind the desire for change. This may be a challenge for you and your partner if often the discussion becomes an argument about whose beliefs and theories are correct. For example, if you say to your partner, "I think James is getting Bs and Cs in school because he is too focused on playing basketball. I think he is too focused on basketball because you are such a basketball fan," your partner may retort, "Grades aren't everything, he is actually well rounded—you should like it that we have the same interests, since that is important." This type of discussion can easily fall into a competition about the best values rather than an airing of these values. A better statement about your concerns might be, "I am concerned about James's getting Bs and Cs in school; I would like for him to get the best grades possible so he has as many options available in the future as possible."

Second, once you are ready to start focusing on solutions, make sure you work hard on defining broad and mutual goals that you agree on. For example, you and your partner may not agree whether your son should get As above all else or be well rounded. Perhaps you can agree that you both want your son to have success in as many areas as possible and have options for the future, which may include both academic and nonacademic pursuits. A set of solutions might focus more on ensuring that he keeps up with assignments, has reasonable study habits, and seeks help when needed rather than on specific targets. Also, weaving in both viewpoints, you and your partner might link participation in sports with a minimum academic standard, which is a common practice in school-based sports programs.

Third, focus mostly on solutions rather than on theories and explanations about the problem. The method of problem solving discussed in chapter 4 emphasizes creativity in coming up with solutions for this reason. Make sure some part of the solution is of interest to your partner. This shows goodwill to your partner and will often lead your partner to take your solutions into account also.

Last, use several discussions to solve a problem, to keep the tensions as low as possible. It is also helpful to make a written note or two about possible solutions, even solutions your partner brings up that do not excite you as much. This will reassure your partner that you are interested in her input and do not want to cover the same ground each time you discuss the problem. Make sure it is clear that no solutions are final, even ones that appear to be working well currently. There is always room for a given solution to be improved in the future, and you or your partner will feel more free to agree to try a solution if both of you know that it can be adjusted if needed.

Final Words

Couples that are successful in reintegrating after a deployment usually make a clear decision to commit their efforts to staying together and working toward a happier relationship. You can work against difficult emotions such as anger and hopelessness by replacing the negative thoughts that fuel them with more realistic ones. More realistic thoughts do not imply blame or include black-and-white thinking but instead describe your problems as unpleasant yet solvable. You can make a lot of progress improving your relationship by making sure your day-to-day experiences are as positive as possible. This includes doing simple but pleasant activities with your partner and also focusing and commenting on your partner's positive behavior. This often encourages each of you to put more importance on enjoying each other and recognizing your individual and couple strengths. When it is necessary to make decisions as a couple or to try to change things, try to build the habit of having frequent and brief talks with your partner. When conflict occurs, you can suggest to your partner to use a time-out, but always propose a time in the near future to resume the discussion more calmly. More difficult problems call for the problem-solving method described in a previous chapter, but make sure that your feelings and values are discussed before trying to tackle the problem with solutions. These problem-resolution methods can be learned, but it takes persistence and patience before they begin to pay off.

Chapter 7

Helping Your Partner Redevelop Relationships with the Kids

"I thought we would all be happy again when Dad came home."

—*Sadie*

One of the biggest concerns you may have in the postdeployment period is how your children are adjusting to your partner's return. Also, you may be struggling with giving up sole control of parenting. During the deployment, caring for your children was likely all on your shoulders, even if you had help from friends and family. Because you want to make sure things go well, some of the conflicts you have with your partner may be about your partner's style of parenting and his sense that you are getting in the way of this.

Your role with your children continues to be very important now that your partner has returned. The focus of this role, however, is different in a couple of ways. First, you and your partner can learn to work better as a team, even when you have very different ideas about or approaches to parenting. Second, you and your partner can provide good examples for your children of how to address problems that arise in the reintegration period. I will discuss the details of these strategies in the second half of this chapter. There are some key things to understand first about child development and adjustment that will help guide you as you and your partner move forward.

What You Need to Know About Reintegration Problems and Kids

At times your view of life as an adult differs from the viewpoints of your children in ways that are hard to imagine. Your children probably changed in obvious ways over the course of your partner's deployment, and in ways much greater than the adults. As I discussed in chapter 1, children of different ages will have different reactions when your partner returns from deployment, and they will also adjust at differing speeds over the following few months. Furthermore, children tend to be egocentric and relate family events directly to themselves, which may lead to the kinds of problems I describe below.

Children's Development Marches On

Your partner will probably comment on how much your children have grown over the time he was deployed. Some of the less obvious changes have to do with the way children think, their interests, and their social behavior. For example, as children reach the teen years, it is typical for them to become more private, talking less about other kids at school or what activities interest them.

You and your partner may notice changes in one or more of your children that seem to coincide with your partner's deployment, and you may believe that these changes are brought about by your partner's absence and return. Although the deployment may have led to some problems, your child's development continues throughout all phases of the deployment from influences unrelated to the deployment. Consider the possibility that the changes you and your partner notice have very little to do with your partner's deployment but would have occurred during that time frame anyway. Another way to look at this is that even if everything in the deployment and in the reintegration period went smoothly, you and your partner would begin in a new starting place with your family when your partner returned. The children cannot start where things left off because their development continued regardless of other events.

Sam and Kathy, for example, noticed that their daughter, Alyssa (age 13), began to communicate less and less with Kathy while Sam was deployed. He complained after his return from South Korea that Alyssa spent more time in her room, texting on her cell phone, and snapped back whenever he asked whether she was finished with her homework. Sam wanted to ground her for her disrespect and not being more part of the family, but both Kathy and Sam thought that she had been through so much with his deployment that they should go easy on her. After talking with their friends and their pediatrician, they realized she may be *just being a teenager*. With this in mind, they began to look into all the other possible ways to deal with Alyssa's teenage behavior to encourage less disrespect and more enjoyable activities with the rest of the family.

What to Expect from Your Children's Adjustment to Reintegration

Children need time to adjust during the period of reintegration just as adults do. Some of these adjustments concern changed routines, expectations, and how you and your partner work together in managing your children's behavior. The time required for your children to adjust to these changes cannot be rushed. This means that there will be many times in which you or your partner think that it has been long enough for a child to begin to accept your partner's discipline or feel more comfortable around him or her. Successful reintegration depends on many individual factors, so there is no set time frame for this adjustment to occur.

In general, count on *at least* six months or more for your children to adjust to the return of your partner, and even longer for your partner and your children to redevelop their relationships. Typically, younger children will adjust more quickly than older children, in part because younger children do well with most parental figures that provide them with warmth, affection, and structure in their lives, regardless of whether they are actually parents. Older children understand and are more aware about what family life has been like, and if they are in their teens, they might have their own expectations of how reintegration should occur. Thus, resist the temptation to think and feel critically when older children have more problems with their returning parent than younger ones. Their greater maturity can result in more difficulty with reintegration rather than less.

Reintegration from Your Child's View and How to Help

You will need to help your children understand problems that occur during the reintegration period in the proper context. For example, children are more likely to believe that they cause events than that adults do, and may believe that what happens in the family is due to their behavior. If you and your partner are not getting along or if your partner is struggling with reintegration in your family, at work, or in other roles, you may find that one or more children take responsibility for things not going well. It may be difficult to know whether this is happening because your child will probably not say directly, "If only I would not act up, you and Daddy would not fight so much." You can help your children understand that a great deal of what happens is not due to their behavior but is instead caused by other factors.

Some children cope with family stress and conflict by working very hard to be a "good child." They do this with the idea that very good behavior on their part will improve how things are going in the household. Although it is always great for your children to listen and be helpful, their positive behavior alone does not make you and your partner work together better, solve your problems, or help your partner adjust. You may notice that when you or your partner is having problems with one child, another tries to do everything right to try to repair the problems in the household. This child is actually carrying a great deal of burden for the unhappiness in the household even though she will not be able to describe it this way. Again, delivering the message to your child that it is not her burden to carry can help lighten your child's load.

Children are also likely to view disagreements between you and your partner and changes in household duties or roles as signals that you and your partner may not stay together. The fear of their parents' breakup is very common among children of all ages. When this fear exists, children also wonder what would happen to them should the breakup occur. Depending on your child's age, you may want to provide some detail about what you and your partner are doing to address problems and changes in the household. For example, you can state that you and your partner are still trying different ways to help the family get along after your partner's return. You can reassure them that you and your partner both love them and that you and he will keep working until everyone gets used to the changes.

You may also struggle with how to help your children when your partner is unhappy and acts in irritable and unpredictable ways. For example, after planning to go as a family to a picnic or some other social event, your partner may abruptly change his mind about going, or snap at other family members while there for almost no reason. These can be frequent and often temporary behaviors of many returning veterans, but they can be upsetting to children. This is particularly true if the behavior is unkind toward you or results in arguments with you. The most important factor is how you respond verbally to your partner when these things occur. You can help your child understand that there is a reason for this behavior but that it is still not okay by asserting yourself in ways described in other chapters. It is important to give your partner feedback about the impact of the behavior on you and your children, as well as to demonstrate that you believe this behavior to be inappropriate by removing yourself from the situation.

In the list below I present some ways of talking to your child about the issues just discussed.

Ways to Talk to Your Child About Change, Problems, and Conflicts

- **Invite a brief discussion with your child if you suspect he is feeling responsible for family problems.** You can say, "I know your father and I fight sometimes, and it upsets you. We don't always agree, and we feel really strongly about a lot of things, including you and your brothers. This does not mean it is your fault that we disagree, or that you can make things better by being super well behaved."

- **Make sure the discussion takes into account your child's worry about the family and what will happen to her.** Younger children are most concerned about whether arguments mean you will separate or divorce. Say, "Even though your father and I argue, we love each other, and you and your brother very much. We are working hard to figure things out so that we can be a happier, more peaceful family."

- **Children, even teenagers, do not need the details about your disagreements, even though they probably already know the general subject of those disagreements.** It is important not to talk to children as if they were your close friends. Doing so causes children of all ages to feel uneasy and can create painful conflicts about whose side to take.

- **Help your child understand possible reasons behind your partner's behavior, without excusing that behavior.** If your partner is dealing with chronic back pain and other issues, you can say that your partner is "dealing with a lot of hard problems since coming home, and pain in his back that won't go away. That doesn't make it okay for him to snap at you or me, and I will keep working with him to find better ways to deal with his pain and other problems."

How to Help Your Partner and Your Children in Reintegration

You can take several actions to help your partner develop a better relationship with your children in the weeks, months, and perhaps years after your partner returns from deployment. Similar to what I have described, the foundation of these methods is to help your partner and your children increase the amount and quality of enjoyable time that they spend together. It also means working together as a team with your partner so that you, as parents, present a united front. This will help your partner return to a full and equal role in your children's eyes.

Spending Time Together

It is important that your partner spend time with your children in activities that are fun for everyone. There are many ways to accomplish this. First, as I discussed above, weekly events can be planned during your regular business meetings or discussions. The family-based events can include anything from movie or game nights to attendance at one of the children's musical performances. Unless your partner is prevented by chronic injury or pain, encourage him to participate in any other leisure activities that your children are interested in, including backyard basketball or baseball, fishing, or computer games. This can be a challenge because the older the child, the more hesitant he or she will be to invite your partner to participate. Many veterans, especially those experiencing combat, do not feel part of the household or family or feel different from civilians in general. Try discussing with your partner that you know these are common barriers that you believe can be overcome in time. You might start by asking, "You may be waiting for Douglas to show that he wants to shoot hoops. Is there anything getting in the way of you taking the first move?"

You can use the skills I presented above to encourage your partner to choose these activities with your children. For example, after spending time with you and your children during movie night, you can let your partner know how much it meant to you, even though you knew at times the children's actions were highly irritating or that the activity went on for too long for him.

If your partner has reasons that any specific activity is uncomfortable because of combat reminders or other deployment factors, you can suggest that he make an adjustment to the activity. I worked with a veteran of the war in Iraq whom I will call Thomas. Thomas enjoyed watching his son play soccer. His time in Iraq, however, had led him to be very wary of young men with international soccer team jerseys, which was the fashion among young men in that area of the world—and young men in Iraq in civilian clothes at the time were also potential combatants. After his return, Thomas had continued to be wary of young men who fit that description. After we discussed this with his partner, Thomas and his wife briefly talked with their son about the issue. They let him know that his discomfort in the soccer arena would sometimes lead Thomas to step out of the arena for a while or walk away from the bleachers. Because their son was a teenager and was curious about why this was necessary, Thomas mentioned that the crowd and the way some of the people were dressed were reminders of combat that led him to feel uncomfortable. This was logical and helpful for their son because it helped him understand his father's standoffish behavior at soccer games.

Reconnecting with Younger Children

It may be harder with children younger than six for you or your partner to know how to connect and spend positive time together. Younger children engage in a lot of imaginary play, and it can sometimes be unclear how to play with them—particularly for your partner, who may not have much recent experience interacting with a young child. Your role can be to model activities that are enjoyable and worthwhile, and to suggest that your partner try the activities to connect with your younger child. It is important to leave cell phones and other distractions aside during the time you or your partner connects with your child. Spending short periods of time together frequently is best; fifteen uninterrupted minutes on most days can make a big difference.

You can start by identifying the types of activities that will be fun for your younger child and feel comfortable and engaging for your partner. The best of these activities focuses much of the attention directly on the child as she is playing. Children communicate a great deal about how they feel and what they are thinking through play. They may not have the ability to express their thoughts and feelings in words. Often these are acted out in their play and expressed from their imagination instead. Also, when a child knows that you are watching and listening to her play, she really feels cared for and this increases her connection with you.

Watching TV and playing video games are the most common things that parents do with younger children when they are unsure what to do, but these activities are passive and do not involve much talking; this limits the connection you can make with your child. In contrast, reading to your child has several benefits. There is some structure to this activity, which will make it easier to get your partner started on increasing time with your child. Start by creating a ritual of reading at the same time each day, in addition to bedtime reading, in order to provide a simple and frequent way to reconnect. After doing this a few times, you can ask your partner to sit with you while you read and then ask your partner to read while you sit with him during this time. Once your child is used to having books read to her, she can bring the book to you or your partner when she is ready and wants to make a connection. If you are unsure of the best books to read for your child, bookstore staff members can help with this question, and online book retailers also provide guidance to the books that will interest your child.

You can also join in an activity alongside your child. For example, if your child is drawing, you can sit with her and draw while she draws. Of course, the quality of your drawing will not matter to her, so resist the temptation to comment on how bad you think your drawing is. Show interest in your child's drawing and show her yours. You can invite your partner to sit with you as you do this. A similar type of activity is playing with your child with blocks, dolls, or action figures. When you decide to be involved this way, make sure you are near your child's level, either on the floor or sitting near her on a low chair or stool. Follow her lead or simply notice out loud what she is doing. For example, you might say, "You are building a tall tower and only using the blue blocks," or "You are giving your baby a bottle and rocking her." This lets your daughter know that she has your undivided attention and builds a strong sense of connection.

When you have developed the habit of observing your child's play, she may invite you (or your partner) to join in. You can respond in a way that allows your child to direct the play. For example, imagine that she brings you a doll she calls Anna and says, "Here, you be Anna." Follow up by asking, "What is Anna doing?" Or if your child gives you a crayon as she is drawing, you can ask, "What should I draw?" In order to allow your child to really express herself and connect with you and your partner, limit your commands or suggestions about how to play or what to draw.

In any of the activities you are watching or doing with your child, it is helpful to provide simple comments to let her know you are noticing what she is doing. For example, you can state, "Oh, I see you're using the red crayon now," or "Now you have the blocks stacked." You do not need to praise or guide your child's play in any way for this to be a way to connect with her. She will notice that you are there even if she does not respond directly, and this will encourage her to continue expressing herself through play. You can begin using this method yourself and after doing it a few times, point out to your partner what you are doing. Emphasize to your partner that even five minutes makes a meaningful difference in the parent-child connection.

How can making simple observations actually make a difference? Imagine that you have a great story to tell about something that happened today and your partner devoted five minutes to listen to your story without interruption. The impact of commenting on your child's play is very similar to this. For a young child, using imagination in play and drawing is a way of trying to understand the world and describing what she thinks to others. Your child is telling stories, figuring things out about the world, and sharing this with you as you pay close attention. A great deal of research has supported this method and shows that it improves the parent-child relationship and behavior of the child (McMahon and Kotler 2008).

If the play behavior becomes destructive or dangerous, such as throwing a toy, you can simply stop the session by getting up, saying, "I think we'll stop for now," and walking away. This is far more powerful over time than any punishment that you might use for broken rules. Your child really appreciates your attention, and your turning away shows her that the attention will stop when she shows unwanted behavior. Intervene only if your child continues a behavior that risks injury, such as pulling on a table cloth with objects on it, as giving more attention to unwanted behavior only makes it more likely to happen in the future.

Guidelines for Connecting to Your Child Through Play

- **Leave your cell phone aside and silent for the period of time.** The TV and other technology should be turned off.

- **Watching TV or playing video games prevents the best forms of connecting.** Try to limit watching TV and playing video games with younger children and use the alternative activities described previously.

- **Reading to your child is a good structured activity for connecting.** Consider reading during the day, in addition to bedtime reading. This is a particularly useful suggestion for your partner.

- **Use a low chair or stool or sit on the floor when joining your child in play.** It is helpful to be on the same physical level as your child to connect emotionally.

- **Join in activities that your child initiated, such as drawing or playing with blocks or action figures.** Your child may ask you to join in; if so, ask your child for direction.

- **Use simple statements to narrate your child's play behavior without additional praise or direction.** Your child appreciates the attention and feels best if he is able to decide freely how to play.

- **Stop the play session if your child begins to do something dangerous or destructive.** You can say, "I think we'll stop for now" and simply get up and walk away. You do not need to punish or talk to your child right at the time he misbehaves unless you need to stop the behavior from being repeated to avoid injury. Any type of attention can in fact make the behavior more likely to occur in the future.

Resist the Desire to Spoil Your Children or Totally Relax Your Expectations

Children thrive on consistency and predictability. You probably feel bad when you see your children upset during the reintegration period, since your children caused none of the changes they have to face. If you do anything special at all for your children after your partner returns, such as offering extra toys, gifts, or privileges, this should be modest and limited to the first few days or weeks after your partner's reunion with you. Over time you may be tempted to relax your expectations of your children at school or around the house, especially if you and your partner are struggling with reintegration issues. It is important to let your children know that you expect them to make the same effort at school as before. Expect your children to be just as much a part of keeping the household running as before such as doing chores, although there are probably some changes because of the tasks that your partner has taken over. This may be a larger challenge if your partner wants to provide special treats and gifts, since he may want to make up for lost time. Discuss with your partner that the biggest gift he can provide your children is time, and encourage doing activities together and play as described above.

Work as a Parenting Team

You have noticed that working as a team is a big theme in this book. In parenting, working as a team is especially important because you get better behavior, it is reassuring to the children, and it is less overall effort. Your partner may complain that the children do not obey him well enough in this period of reintegration. You can let your partner know that working together at first will let the kids know that you support your partner's role as a parent and expect that they respond the same way to each of you. Over time, you can step back more as your children grow more comfortable with your partner providing directions, giving commands, or working on problems with your children.

As an example, if you have been taking your child to soccer practice, you can suggest that both of you go for a few times. When asking your children to clean their rooms, you can suggest that the two of you supervise the task together, check up on progress, and provide feedback. Resist the temptation to comment on your partner's way of parenting at this point, especially if it may undermine him in the view of your children.

Present a United Front

You and your partner will have a much easier time with parenting the more you can appear united in your decisions. You provide less chance for your children to drive a wedge between the two of you by asking each of you separately for permission for an activity. Be willing to put off a decision when a request comes separately until you are able to talk to your partner about it. Most of the time decisions are not as pressing as your children may think. You can also institute a general rule that requests, such as plans to socialize with friends, should come a day in advance of the event to allow that consultation with your partner.

It is important that you and your partner work out parenting disputes away from your children's hearing. It is best to let your partner know in advance that you do not want to disagree in front of your children mostly because they will respond better to your parenting if they are not often witnessing disagreement. You can suggest to your partner when a disagreement becomes apparent, "Maybe this is something for our meeting later on. We want to give Claire a full discussion on this issue."

Use "we" language to show your children that the two of you are a united front. Examples include, "We want you to..." or "We've decided that you..." In order to convince your partner that you want to work as a team, try volunteering to deliver a decision to your child or children, even when you conceded on the issue. For example, imagine you and your partner decided that the kids would not visit with their friends on Saturday afternoon or night because of family social events on top of homework and chores. You might suggest to your partner, "I don't mind telling the kids about this. They may guess who favored which decision, and I want them to know it was *us* who made the decision." Be sure to use *we* in talking with the children to present the plans.

Final Words

Your children continued developing even when your partner was away, so changes you and your partner observe may be independent of the deployment. Changes that are due to the deployment, however, often require at least six months of adjustment time. Children tend to interpret events in their own way, including taking responsibility on themselves for how your family is getting along. You play an important role in helping your children understand some of the challenges your family faces by talking with them about what they observe.

You can help your partner redevelop his relationship with your children by taking the same positive approach as I described for your own relationship with your partner. Some one-on-one time with your children is also important, and for younger children this can include playing in an activity your child enjoys, which allows a chance for undivided attention from you or your partner. Because this approach is probably different from other types of play that you and your partner may be used to, consider trying it and showing your partner the method. In general, using teamwork with your partner will help your partner resume his full role as a parent, and also result in more effective parenting.

Chapter 8

Special Challenges and Getting Support

"I am getting no help from him with the kids or work around the house—I can't do this all by myself!"

—Monique

I t is helpful to identify factors that are beyond your control in the reintegration period after deployment. This chapter focuses on a limited number of these circumstances, but the list of unforeseen things that may happen to you and your partner could be longer. It may help to understand these issues in more detail. In the last part of this chapter I describe some of the factors to consider when seeking support and encouragement from others.

Challenges in Reintegration

There are several key challenges to reintegration that I review below. Your partner may be unwilling or unable to work cooperatively with you, despite your best efforts to invite him to do so. This may be based on injuries, both seen and unseen, that your partner received as part of military service. For many people, it is helpful to identify the source of the problem, even if you cannot change the situation. Some issues, such as chronic pain and being in a dual-military family, are challenges that both of you face, and I present some suggestions for dealing with them.

When Your Partner Will Not, or Cannot, Collaborate with You

I have discussed several ways to try to engage your partner in a productive working relationship to have a successful reintegration into your family. When you have asked your partner to talk regularly about problems in the household or to plan consistent family outings, your partner may have resisted, become angry, or simply withdrew. This lack of cooperation may also have come in the form of a refusal to talk about an argument. It may be helpful to take five minutes to consider why this is so. Make a list of the top five reasons that your partner will not or cannot collaborate with you below.

Example: *My partner gets too upset to talk calmly about money.*

1. _____

2. _____

3. _____

4. _____

5. _____

Your reasons may likely be true, but based on my and others' clinical experiences with veterans struggling with their partners, I recommend considering other factors also. *Working* on a relationship may be a foreign idea for your partner. Your partner may never have been faced with the necessity of looking closely at a relationship to consider how it should change for the better to handle a new source of stress. Many people have a sense that intimate relationships that continue are "meant to be" and that you must wait and endure to see whether your own relationship is in that category. It is hard to convince someone with this belief that a few changes in how each partner chooses to respond to a problem may lead to a great deal more happiness. As I have mentioned, when your partner is concerned about autonomy, or making independent decisions outside of any influence of others, it can be hard to engage him in a teamwork style of working on problems.

An additional issue is that the process of going from a career in the military to a civilian life is an overwhelming process for many veterans who have recently returned from a deployment and then separated from active duty. It is possible that your partner is having difficulty focusing on issues with your family and at the same time is dealing with a change in career and an identity as a civilian. You can gain a greater appreciation for the point of view of your partner by reading *Courage After Fire*, by Keith Armstrong and coauthors (2006).

Trauma experienced by your partner in the course of military service is another barrier to improving how you and your partner handle reintegration. I will discuss in chapter 9 getting treatment for the traumas associated with combat experiences. Resistance to dealing with these problems is common, but I will also describe some of the resources available that may help you support your partner in making the decision to get professional help.

Pain, Injury, and Disability

Your partner may suffer from chronic pain and chronic injuries and be limited by these problems. He may have sought a disability determination from the Department of Veterans Affairs to receive payment for this disability. These are tough challenges that go beyond the concrete problems of pain and a reduced ability to work. These injuries and the resulting disability affect how military service members and veterans view how worthwhile they are, their roles in life, and how they relate to others.

For example, consider Evan, a veteran from Iraq who was receiving treatment from his local VA for post-traumatic stress disorder and traumatic brain injury that affected his concentration and led to light sensitivity. He had been evaluated by the VA and received monthly payments for some of these injuries, but appealed the benefit decision and continued to seek greater benefits because he felt that his concentration and light sensitivity continued to prevent him from working. Evan found this to be a consuming job itself, with long delays before a decision would be made. He also felt that the potentially larger monthly disability payment was due to him, given his sacrifice. His struggle left him unable to make plans with his wife, Sharon, to buy a house, and he found through trying to prove his disability that others saw him as avoiding working. Sharon complained that he was stuck and unable to develop a network of friends or decide what his next step in life would be.

Another veteran of Afghanistan, Iraq, and earlier conflicts, Neil, was dealing with recurring back and knee pain from several injuries he received while serving in the infantry as a sniper and also in special operations. Even at age forty-three, Neil used a cane to support himself as he walked. The pain had gradually increased, and as he explored various jobs, he found little he could do. His wife, Elaine, was aware on the days that his pain was worse and frequently asked whether the pain was bothering him. Neil had little desire to focus on his pain and was often irritated at the question. He did not see himself as disabled but was not sure what he could do. He felt adrift and rudderless, and most of his days were spent taking his kids to school, various functions, and sports practices, a role he did not really enjoy.

If your partner has chronic pain and feels limited in his role, it may be helpful to think about how to relate to your partner. What is your goal for trying to help? Chronic pain is a fact of life that your partner has to deal with, but are you focused on constantly trying to alleviate this pain? Have you asked your partner what he wants you to do to be helpful in coping with it? Your partner may struggle with feeling unable to fulfill his role as your partner, as a parent, and as a provider but may be unable to say this to you directly. Perhaps the most important role you can play is to be willing to listen to your partner talk about this struggle when he is ready without trying to change a situation that is essentially unchangeable.

Besides being a good listener, there is a more active role that you can occasionally take. Your partner may seek fewer chances to be social or active because of the concern that pain will get in the way as that social event continues beyond his endurance. You can continue to offer the opportunities to be social and encourage participation in family events. If your partner wishes you to be involved in ongoing medical care, this can be a useful way that you can show support even though you are not actually changing anything.

Dual-Military Career Issues

You and your partner may have both served in the military. There are benefits to this as well as challenges. You benefit by having an inside view of the military and share in your partner's understanding of the military. You and your partner do not need to explain to each other what it means to be involved and share in the culture of the military as well as the impact the experience has had on your life as a whole.

At the same time, your experience could have been very different from your partner's experience. In addition, as in any relationship, you and your partner may have decided that one person's career in the military takes priority and made certain choices about assignments and opportunities to allow this to occur. On the other hand, you may not have discussed how your careers would evolve. Or you may have experienced other stresses because of the clashes between your careers. What are the top five issues having to do with your careers that deserve discussion now that your partner has returned from deployment? Take some time to list these, and use the communication skills discussed in chapter 4 to begin working through them.

Military Career Issues to Discuss with Your Partner

Example: *We assumed that my partner's career would be more important than mine, but didn't really talk about what I would do once I left the military.*

1. _____

2. _____

3. _____

4. _____

5. _____

Taking Care of Yourself and Getting Support

There are many challenges you will face in reintegration that require patience and consistent effort. You may not feel that your partner is working well with you to tackle these problems. This part of the chapter will focus on specific ways you can get help and support and improve your outlook by making sure you feel as positive and energetic as possible during this time.

Self-Care

Self-care is a popular term among psychologists who study the ways in which patients participate in their own medical care. The term is usually meant to include eating a healthy diet, taking medications as prescribed by a doctor, and noticing symptoms of illness that are important to monitor. I use the term a little differently here, starting with a description of other ways to care for yourself better and then discussing the complications of involving family members as part your self-care.

Self-Care by Increasing Individual Happiness

I presented several ways to buffer stress in previous sections by using more realistic and less hopeless ways of thinking. But one of the best methods of taking care of yourself is to make sure that your home is not the only place you get enjoyment and fulfillment. There are many ways this can be done, which varies from person to person. For example, Anne decided that since things are so tense at home, she would get together once a week for a couple of hours with her girlfriends. This was not a problem for Michael, her husband, who was a veteran of both the Gulf War I in Iraq and the second war in Iraq. She arranged to do this after the couple attended their weekly educational program at the local vet center. She often invited him to go to these get-togethers with her, but most of the time he refused. Other possibilities might include social events through your church or spending time with a sibling. You may need to devote some effort to list all of the possible activities that would bring some pleasure and then work out with your partner how they might fit into your lives on a regular basis. Take care not to imply blame for your need to find an activity outside your home on the problems caused by your partner's return. Reintegration can be difficult work from time to time, and both you and your partner could benefit from having another source of fun or enjoyment than family-related activities.

In the next chapter I will review indicators for individual treatment such as psychotherapy, but it is important to say here that psychotherapy and other types of treatment are valuable ways of taking care of yourself. Entering into treatment is a personal decision, but there are some reasons some partners avoid treatment in the reintegration period. Emily had been working in couples therapy with her partner, Rodrigo, for several months. She had been in individual therapy in the past because she sometimes had problems with depression, but she felt that their current problems came from the combat experiences that Rodrigo had had in Afghanistan. Rodrigo did not agree with this, and Emily was afraid that her starting therapy gave him the idea that the problem was hers and not his. Making a decision to get help with her depression was blocked by her belief that Rodrigo would use this to support his point of view. Unfortunately, Emily had the opportunity to accomplish two things—she could have possibly been happier if she improved her mood through treatment, and she missed the chance to show Rodrigo a good example of how to be happier and improve the relationship.

Extended Family and Self-Care

Family members can be a source of additional pleasure and support outside of your relationship. This can be complicated by past issues in those relationships as well as by more recent events that occurred around the deployment and homecoming. Janet is the wife of an army veteran who arranged to have a week alone with Kevin in their apartment when he returned from deployment. She made sure they were not interrupted by visits with his parents. Kevin's parents continued to be hurt about the event, since they were able to spend previous reunions from deployment with their son before Janet and Kevin were together. Janet had been close to his parents, but contact with them became strained for months following Kevin's return. This was difficult for Janet since she did not have any close friends near her.

Another issue to be careful with is talking with close family members about issues you and your partner are struggling with. Although it may seem natural for you to talk with your close family about the things you are trying to accomplish with your partner, remember that your partner may have a different idea about what is private and what is acceptable to discuss with family members. Refer back to chapter 5 about the possibility that your partner's habits gained from training and deployment experiences may have made him more likely to withhold information. In addition, consider recent and past history among you, your partner, and your extended family for clues about what is fair game to discuss. You can also consider having a discussion with your partner about your need to talk with someone outside your family. This will give your partner the benefit of letting you know which family members he is most and least comfortable sharing details about your family situation with.

Getting Support from the Military and Veteran Community

At times your best option for gaining support are from those most familiar with your situation, including those involved in the military and veteran support community. There are benefits to these associations, including common experiences and goals, as well as some reasons for avoiding working them. I discuss these factors below.

Considerations for Military and Veteran Community Support

You are probably aware that there is a robust community of support made up of spouses and other family members of service members and veterans of military service. This support comes in the form of organized family-readiness programs within the military as well as nonprofit organizations created by veterans and family members of veterans. An online search of the terms "military veterans, family, support" yields a number of such groups. Other people whose partners are also deployed in military service can understand your situation in a way that few others can. The benefits of these connections are that you can commit yourself to supporting the well-being of families like your own and service members and veterans like your partner, especially when you feel you are at a standstill with your own partner. I list several of the more well-established groups in chapter 9.

There are also some reasons to avoid the official and non-profit support structures. If you have been part of family-readiness groups or other organized family networks while your partner was deployed, you may have found some complications when news about personnel or family issues traveled quickly among members of the network. This can produce conflict between you and your partner. If you and your partner are struggling with reintegration issues, you may want to think carefully about whom you confide in about your family.

The Online Community

Online social media services, including Facebook and Twitter, are some of the most common mutual support methods. Many of the nonprofit groups developed by veterans and family members of veterans use these tools to connect with each other and offer support. These are valuable and powerful networking tools that can connect you to others who are in the same situation. I have noticed some posts that have a form similar to "Yes, my wife is really dealing with PTSD issues, too. Just last night…" Many users of these social media systems do not realize how public these messages are. Revealing personal information in a public forum is likely to be highly upsetting to your partner. Consider making direct contact with those in that social network if you would like to gain support from others who are dealing with problems similar to your own.

Final Words

Your partner may not be willing to work with you to improve how the two of you relate in this period of reintegration after a military deployment. This may occur for a range of reasons, and it may be helpful to understand the reasons from your partner's point of view. Although this can be upsetting, it may also not be permanent, so one way of dealing with this is to make sure you have enough support from others during this period of time. An important factor in remaining motivated and positive is joining friends or relatives in activities that are enjoyable. At the same time, it would be important to invite your partner to join you in social events every now and then, as well as to coordinate with you on your efforts to help the family work well during the period of reintegration. The military or veteran community is a natural place for you to seek support because of the common experiences, but at times the community also may feel too close. Finally, some judgment is necessary when communicating online, since most people are not aware of how public such messages are.

Chapter 9

When Do We Go for Help?

"We just did not think things were so bad that we needed to go for help—everyone goes through tough times, and I've seen couples who were worse off get through it without therapy."

—*Aileen*

One of the most difficult decisions for many people is whether to seek professional help. Often the question about treatment you may ask yourself comes in the following form: "Am I doing so badly that I need to see a professional?" or "Are we so close to splitting up that we need to see a counselor?" The decision itself to get help may be seen as a sign of the status of things. If you (or your relationship) need a professional, you may take it as meaning that you (or your relationship) have hit rock bottom.

There are some reasons that the decision to get help should not be taken as a sign of how poorly you are doing. When this decision is taken as a sign, it tends to make you feel worse about how well you are doing—it increases your pessimism, hopelessness, and despair. These feelings are not helpful for improving your life or relationship, and indeed, they may tend to drain your energy for improving things. Also, viewing the decision to get help as a sign of how badly you are doing is based on stigma, or the idea that poor psychological or relationship health is an embarrassment, a failure, and a sign of weakness. This is unfortunate, since you and your partner have endured enormous stress, and in the reintegration period you have faced the type of changes that only a fraction of other couples and families have ever faced. I will discuss more about stigma and how it affects you and your partner in the pages to come, but first I want to discuss more useful signs that you can use to make your decision to get help.

What Are the Signs We Need Help?

The basic yardstick used by mental health professionals for seeking help is based on *daily functioning*. By this, we mean how you are doing in your daily activities, duties, and relationships with others. For example, if certain symptoms, such as feelings of depression or anxiety, prevent you from completing your every-day tasks, such as getting to work or taking care of chores, then these symptoms are interfering with daily functioning. When these symptoms have an impact for a consistent period of time regardless of your efforts, then this is the sign for most people that it is time to get some sort of assistance. Below I discuss more specifics about types of signs you or your partner might see that would lead you to this decision, as well as to how this applies to relationships.

Individual Signs

Most of the individual signs include common feelings that we all have—feelings of anxiety, depression or low mood, and apathy. Symptoms of depression also include changes in appetite, such as eating significantly more than is typical for a consistent period of time or having so low an appetite that you lose more than five or ten pounds. Indecision and lack of concentration also can be symptoms of depression, especially if they are not common for you. You may also have thoughts of harming your-self or ending your life that occur when you are feeling these other symptoms. There are various forms of depression and anxiety disorders, and each involves somewhat different combinations of symptoms. If you are wondering whether you have one of these problems, there are many online surveys you can take. One of the best sources of online screening is offered by the nonprofit Screening for Mental Health Inc. at the website http://www.mentalhealthscreening.org.

If you have symptoms consistent with clinical depression or anxiety or some other problem, you may also be asked whether these symptoms interfere with your day-to-day activities and tasks. Although this is the most important question, less attention and time are usually given to understanding this part of the symptoms. Consider answering the following questions about how you have been feeling for the past several weeks.

	Every Day	Some Days	Never
1. Because of my mood or other feelings, I get much less work completed than I used to.			
2. I am less motivated to start a project or to finish a project that I have already started.			
3. I get less enjoyment from TV shows, books, or other types of entertainment than I used to.			
4. I have less interest in seeing my friends because of how I have been feeling.			
5. I get into more arguments with family members because of my feelings, attitudes, and actions.			

Each of the experiences in the quiz above involves how your symptoms keep you from being productive, enjoying life, or enjoying your relationships. If you indicated *every day* on more than one item on the quiz above, then your symptoms are probably getting in the way of your life. This is different from struggling with a particular problem that makes you feel tired or defeated from time to time. If this struggle produces problems in many areas of your life on a regular basis because of the way it makes you feel, then it may be the time to get professional help.

For example, Elena was having difficulty with Juan because his injuries from his service in Iraq left him with back pain every day. He was irritable with her and their children, and they argued frequently about money, the amount of time he spent with his army buddies, and his lack of choosing a new career or school since he left active duty. Elena believed she had approached Juan with respect and encouragement about these problems, but he was not willing to discuss them without being angry. She could not concentrate well at work and was easily upset when people asked how the couple had been doing since Juan's return. She avoided her friends because of the embarrassment of her situation. Elena came to realize she was depressed, even though she did not believe she was the source of their problems. She was not feeling motivated and positive enough to come up with a way to solve the challenges they faced. She loved Juan and did not want the way she currently felt to make her less understanding of what he went through or to not have the ability to help them out of their current situation.

How do you know if your partner is experiencing problems with depression, anxiety, or some other problem with mood? Perhaps you are concerned about your partner's use of alcohol. You will not be able to diagnose your partner and convince him to get treatment based on this, but it will be helpful to become aware of the specific symptoms that your partner might show that can interfere with his daily life. You can use the educational resources suggested below or the screening website mentioned previously to help you and your partner identify these symptoms.

Some of the classic symptoms of post-traumatic stress disorder may be interfering with your partner's progress in reintegration. I described in chapter 5 the experience of hypervigilance, which is an intensive attention to anything in one's surroundings that may be a threat. It may lead to avoidance of situations that prompt this hypervigilance. Your partner may show this after he has served in combat; it may resolve after some weeks or months in noncombat or nonmilitary settings, or persist beyond that. You can find full descriptions of PTSD on the website of the National

Center for PTSD of the Department of Veterans Affairs (http://www.ptsd.va.gov).

When do hypervigilance, avoidance, and other reactions to combat become a problem? Think about the adjustments you may be asked, or required, to make by your partner when entering a restaurant. If your partner often refuses to eat in a restaurant because the only "safe" seat is not available, then this may be an indicator of a larger problem. Consider how much and how often you or other family members are inconvenienced by these concerns and how much it disrupts family life.

I worked for several months with an army veteran, Niall, who had advanced training and experience as a sniper. He reported that he almost always entered a new building by scanning high perches, blind entrances, and other recesses that could constitute a position that an adversary might choose for his or her work. He also described calculating escape routes and procedures as another common reflex. His training was likely a strong influence in how he thought about entering buildings and where he sat; for some period of time, he went to his college class early so he could claim the seat with the best defensive position. After some adjustment, this concern faded. He will likely always go through the same thought processes when entering new places, but this becomes a behavior worthy of treatment only if it makes it difficult for him to function in daily life, is distressing to him, or is a disruption for others close to him.

High alcohol use is sometimes a method of coping for service members returning from deployment, and at times it is specifically a way to deal with the anxiety from combat trauma. Alcohol abuse is more common than other drug abuse because of the severe penalties in the military for the use of illegal drugs. The usual guidelines developed over years of research indicate that for men, drinking more than fourteen drinks over one week and more than four on any single day may signal an unhealthy level of drinking. These figures are lower for women—over seven drinks a week or three per day may be a problem. About 25 percent of those who drink over this limit probably already drink at a level defined as alcohol abuse or have a dependence on alcohol. The most common ways alcohol can produce problems include increasing the chances of arguments; physical fights or other types of disruption in the family; problems that occur with drinking and driving, such as legal problems and accidents; and long-term risk of greater health problems. More information about alcohol abuse can be found in the educational resources listed at the end of this chapter.

You may also have a concern about whether your child's behavior problems or unhappiness are reasons for seeking treatment for your child or for your family. For children, obvious signs that mood or behavior problems interfere in daily life include problems at school or with peers, or disruptions in sleeping or eating. Another indicator that your child's mood or behavior is interfering with daily life is that your whole family begins to revolve around the child in an effort to keep her from becoming upset and to have her continue to be happy and well behaved. For example, you may feel you are always walking on eggshells so that your child does not have a conflict with your partner over rules your partner is attempting to enforce. This may indicate the need to seek treatment for your child and your family because of problems in the relationship between your child and partner.

Relationship Signs

None of the well-researched tests of relationship health provide a clear guide for making the decision to seek help as a couple. Usually such measures will tell you how happy or unhappy your relationship is relative to others and what areas of your relationship, such as support or communication, are stronger or weaker. The decision to get treatment for your relationship is a very personal one and is more complicated than individual treatment because it takes both of you. Here are some guidelines that might help.

Consistent Unhappiness

Consider your overall judgment of happiness in your relationship by answering the following question, which was inspired by the Couples Satisfaction Index (Funk and Rogge 2007): What is your degree of happiness, all things considered, of your relationship? If your answer is "a little unhappy" or "extremely unhappy" or somewhere in between, consider how long this has been true. Your personal decision about treatment hinges, in part, on how long you feel you can tolerate your relationship being a source of stress rather than a source of pleasure and support. For some people a month of unhappiness is too long, but others can tolerate a year or longer because of the other supports and sources of happiness in their lives.

Difficulty Resolving Conflict

The length of time you and your partner take to make up after an argument is an indicator of how well the two of you work together as a couple. In this case I am referring to how quickly you and your partner return to relating normally, not whether you made a decision about how to handle a disagreement.

Making up is actually the same as making a bid for intimacy (chapter 3) in which you and your partner decide to set aside being angry or distant and begin to deal in a normal way with one another. I worked recently with a couple, Renée and William, who had serious arguments about twice a month. Afterward, they did not talk to each other for a week. It became clear that what they really meant was that they had only as much conversation as necessary to manage details of their lives with their nine-year-old son. After Renée would make a couple of attempts at conversation throughout the week, each of them were ready to sit down and talk calmly about the argument. Although they often did not solve the problem they had argued about, they felt somewhat better because they could tell the other what they were upset about. We talked about how much time they spent angry in a typical month and unable to feel the benefits of being a couple: support, fun, sex, and so on. Other couples are able to get to the point of discussing the argument calmly within a half a day or even as soon as two hours. If the time you and your partner spend angry with one another is extended because it takes several days to return to a normal conversational tone, then consider getting professional help.

Difficulty Making Decisions

When you and your partner argue and spend time not talking with each other in a normal way, then it may be difficult to reach a decision on one or several important issues. If you are not able to reach decisions in a mutually satisfying way, then it is not possible to move ahead in the reintegration period after deployment. The reintegration period is often a time of transition for couples, including decisions about starting school, changing jobs, relocating, or having your first (or another) child. It may be useful to seek help if this is true about your relationship. Note, however, that many couples look for a "referee" to decide who is correct about a tough issue, such as whether to relocate. This type of help can be harmful since it replaces your and your partner's judgment and needs with those of a third partner. Second, the best type of therapy will help you and your partner learn how to make decisions so you can continue to make well-formed decisions in the future.

Interference of Your Relationship Problems in Your Daily Life

Consider seeking help when problems in your relationship at home have an effect on work or other aspects of daily life for an extended period of time. Some hidden examples might include inability to concentrate at work because you are upset or preoccupied with your arguments with your partner, worry about how your partner is working with your kids at home while you are at work, and inability to agree on and manage schedules with the kids and their activities, leading to infrequent family meals. Another sign of interference would be that you and your partner turn down chances to socialize as a couple because you believe you will argue prior to the event and not want to attend or not enjoy it because you are currently feuding with one another.

Physical Conflicts and Other Similar Problems

Throwing things during a fight, pushing or restraining your partner, and your partner restraining you while in conflict are all too common. It may be a surprise that professionals classify these as acts of violence, and each has at least some risk of harm. They are signs that some type of professional help is needed. The type of help, however, depends on several factors. First, couple therapy is appropriate only under some conditions when there is physical violence. If the level of violence is low (pushing or throwing things) and has not led to physical injury that requires medical attention, then standard couples or marriage therapy may be relatively safe. In this situation, your therapist should help you and your partner reduce or eliminate these types of behaviors quickly.

If you or your partner is frequently afraid of the other, physical conflict or violence is more of a problem. It is often not possible to treat a couple with that problem with standard relationship therapy, because one of the partners is not able to speak openly to the therapist about what happens at home for fear of revenge from the other spouse. In some cases, one partner may feel afraid or controlled in other ways. Sometimes this comes in the form of one partner's pressure on the other to stay away from friends or family, limits on access to household money, or threats that harm will come to pets or even children as a way to achieve control over the other partner. In each of these situations in which fear is a factor, community-based resources for battering are likely to be more useful and are described more in the "Getting Help" section in this chapter.

Violence can also occur when combat veterans reexperience some version of the trauma they faced during deployment. I have worked with several veterans who saw combat in Iraq or Afghanistan and reported some type of violent behavior once they returned home that occurred in the middle of a nightmare. In one instance, Saul reported that his wife, Helen, woke him up in the middle of the night when he had his hands around her neck. He was horrified and ashamed by this, since they argued but had never been violent with each other. This type of behavior is frequently part of a larger set of PTSD symptoms and could be effectively treated by therapies designed to treat PTSD.

Getting Help

It may feel overwhelming to imagine how to search for treatment, but fortunately you can find some assistance in the process. It is helpful if you know the kinds of things that might get in the way and what to do about those barriers. I discuss below the sources of some resistance, ways to approach your partner about treatment, and types of treatment and other resources.

Barriers: Stigma and Denial

Many people are reluctant to seek treatment because of the stigma of mental health problems. Psychological symptoms are seen by some as a sign of weakness or as a character defect. You may feel this way, or you may suspect that your partner feels this way. Others deny that the symptoms they experience are more than normal stresses and say they do not have time to indulge in treatment, seeing it as a selfish activity. Mental health problems that interfere with daily functioning are actually very common, and often people who are under stress are more prone to experience these problems.

You are likely aware that many active duty service members and reserve or National Guard members feel it is best to deal privately with mental health concerns because they are seen as a risk to one's career. All of the military service branches have attempted to change such attitudes about the importance of recognizing mental health issues and obtaining treatment. But the common perception of many service members is that a direct reaction to disclosing mental health symptoms is being sidelined from responsibilities, losing access to weapons, and being separated from one's unit for treatment purposes when the unit continues to train or prepare for deployment. Stepping back from current responsibilities may indeed be an important step in treatment, so any immediate impact of seeking treatment should be compared to the benefits of treatment through the relief from individual distress and family problems. As you bring the idea of treatment to your partner, be prepared to discuss the potential benefit of this relief.

Talking to Your Partner About Treatment

There are several possible approaches to talking to your partner about treatment. First, consider using the communication skills discussed in previous chapters to let your partner know what you observe and what you are specifically concerned about. Carl, a veteran of the Iraq War, realized the value of his partner's feedback about how he was coming across to others, the effect of his withdrawal, and his avoidance to recognizing how things were going in the family. He reluctantly stated that he needed his wife's view to remind him how things worked in civilian life.

Second, you can recommend to your partner video resources that share how other veterans experienced traumatic deployment. At the VA website, http://www.maketheconnection.net, you and your partner can hear stories recorded by US military veterans and their family members about their military experiences, the emotional pain they went through, and how they decided to seek treatment. In another useful video available on YouTube, Heidi Kraft describes her work with the US Marine Corps as a psychologist in 2004 in Iraq near Fallujah. She met with scores of marines in the midst of the trauma that so often leads to PTSD and describes the effects of her own trauma after she returned from this deployment.

You can also recommend to your partner to read the educational material available on the National Center for PTSD and to conduct a self-screening. This will help your partner examine whether he is experiencing these symptoms without feeling compelled to resist you. As I have discussed throughout this book, it is important to clearly say to your partner that although you have your opinions and concerns, you recognize that it is his own choice about treatment.

If you want more help in communicating with your partner about your concerns, you can contact the national VA call center called Coaching Into Care (888-823-7458, http://www .va.gov/coachingintocare). This free telephone-based service is staffed by mental health professionals who can talk with you about ways to start the conversation with your partner about your concerns. The service is tailored to your specific needs in the discussions you have with your partner, with no limit on the number of consultations you can have.

Supporting Recovery

You likely know you have several additional roles if you are supporting your partner's recovery from emotional injuries from deployment, but you may not know exactly what those roles might be. I describe the ways you can best help your partner as he works with professionals in treatment.

Educate Yourself About the Issues

Use the resources mentioned above and in the section "Finding Support and Treatment" later in this chapter to understand as much as you can about common reactions to combat trauma and other stresses your partner has faced in deployment. This will help you reduce the sense of confusion and alarm that you may feel when you observe your partner become irritated or overwhelmed in crowded social situations, or as a result of other stressors that may be specific to your partner. Consider that this information is for your own benefit—it is not helpful to become a source of education for your partner since that may feel annoying or controlling to him. If you want your partner to know some of the things that you learned about combat reactions, PTSD, or other topics, suggest to your partner what these resources are and let him make the decision to examine them.

Be Part of Your Partner's Treatment

If your partner has started treatment or is preparing to start treatment, it is a good idea to offer to be part of it. There are several ways this can work. First, you can offer to go with your partner to appointments whenever you can, even you if you only sit in the waiting room. Just your presence can be supportive; and if your partner wants to discuss his experience in treatment, you can be available to listen. Second, when your partner's treatment provider wants to gain another opinion about how your partner is doing outside the sessions, it may be helpful to join the session. Remember, however, that when you join your partner's session, the main goal of treatment is still to help your partner. If you want to start therapy for your relationship, you can speak to your partner and his provider in order to get a referral for a different provider. Third, your partner's provider might ask you to play a supportive role in treatment if your partner is being treated for PTSD. For example, the therapist may ask you to support your partner in confronting situations that he avoids due to PTSD symptoms. I discuss ways you can accomplish this in the next section.

Promoting Interaction and Reducing Avoidance

One of the key symptoms of PTSD is avoidance, including avoidance of reminders of combat or situations that involve crowds of people in which potential threats are difficult to detect. Common examples for those who were deployed to urban combat situations, for example, include roadside trash, fireworks or other loud noises, and malls or other crowded venues. If these situations continue to be avoided, your partner's anxious reaction becomes even stronger. This becomes a vicious circle in which the more situations are seen as anxiety provoking, the more power they have to lead to avoidance. By helping your partner avoid situations that make him uncomfortable, you will be unwittingly supporting the development of worse anxiety and worry about these situations (Monson, Fredman, and Adair 2008).

You can help reduce the power of these situations by encouraging your partner to safely and slowly challenge them. As stated above, if your partner is being treated for PTSD, this may be a productive way you can support him in treatment. Start by having a conversation with your partner about supporting him in getting used to some things that you know are uncomfortable. If you have not been part of your partner's treatment, ask about the types of tasks outside the session that he has discussed with the treatment provider, and the ways you can support him.

For your own purposes, list the top places or activities that you and your partner have started to avoid since he returned due to anxiety or worry. You can do this task with your partner if he shows willingness and is agreeable to the discussion. Your partner may have a sense of embarrassment or shame, since avoidance is difficult to understand when compared to the life-threatening situations that most service members face on combat deployments. It is important to treat these concerns with seriousness and your partner with respect even though the avoidance of these situations may not make sense to either of you. It is helpful to make the list with the most difficult items at the top and the easiest at the bottom. If you are not creating the list with your partner, you may not know exactly what would be most and least difficult, but do your best.

Top Places You and Your Partner Avoid Because of Your Partner's Discomfort

Examples:

Football games

Driving in parts of town with lots of roadside trash

1. _____

2. _____

3. _____

4. _____

5. _____

After making the list, suggest to your partner that you do one of these activities or enter one of the situations listed. Remember that your partner must feel that you are not limiting his choice about doing these activities. You might emphasize that both of you are aware that anything that feels difficult at first becomes easier over time. Think about this task extending for several weeks or even months for the most uncomfortable items on the list. It is most effective to stay in these situations for longer periods of time, but be willing to leave if your partner wants to leave and this is a situation that used to be avoided entirely. Any forward progress is positive, even if it is for less time than you wished. For example, I talked about Colin in chapter 5, who refused to attend parties and cookouts because of his concern that he would be asked difficult questions about his service, his anger would erupt, and he would use excessive force. He was afraid that he could not slow down his quick temper as his anxiety at these events increased. After discussing the problem with his wife, Julie, they decided that at first they would go only to smaller family get-togethers, and then later add in larger parties and leave before too many guests drank to excess. Making gradual steps forward is more important than the actual speed of the progress.

Types of Support and Help

You and your partner can obtain help in many ways. I discuss below just a sampling of the main types of help and where you can get educational information, help, and treatment.

Finding Support and Treatment

If your partner is still an active duty service member, you likely have a range of supports and services you are already aware of, depending on the branch of service. Unfortunately, it is still true that those who are legally married have the greatest access to support and care due to the definitions of dependent family members within the Department of Defense. A call to Military OneSource (800-342-9647, http://www.militaryonesource.mil) would be a good start. Unmarried intimate partners of active service members who have been deployed should consider the range of online resources listed below.

The US Department of Veterans Affairs (http://www.va.gov) has a range of services at major medical centers for military veterans, as well as vet centers that provide counseling and education specifically for combat veterans and their family members (http://www.vetcenter.va.gov). Community-based outpatient clinics extend the reach of the VA medical centers in many geographic areas.

A number of nongovernmental organizations have developed services for veterans and their families. Give an Hour (http://www.giveanhour.org) is a clearinghouse of mental health providers willing to provide one hour per week to a military service member, veteran, or family member. This can be a good step for a one- or two-session consultation regarding your situation, and through some providers you may have an opportunity to obtain treatment outside the system of military or VA providers. Be sure to discuss the amount and length of services provided since providers vary regarding their ability to provide treatment.

Other organizations offer outdoor respite and rehabilitative programs designed for military veterans rather than programs that are psychotherapeutic in nature. Although these programs may not directly treat an issue you may feel is a main factor in your or your partner's distress, sometimes participation in these programs can be a first step toward acknowledging problems and resolving them. The Wounded Warrior Project (http://www .woundedwarriorproject.org) has a range of programs to support combat veterans and their family members, including family support retreats and rehabilitative programs for injured veterans. The Iraq and Afghanistan Veterans of America (http://www .IAVA.org) has a number of national legislative initiatives but also provides consultation for navigating the health and benefits systems in the Department of Veterans Affairs. The Disabled American Veterans (http://www.DAV.org) also has legislative initiatives, but in many facilities, DAV volunteers provide transportation to medical facilities for veterans.

Types of Treatment

The most recommended psychotherapy, or talk therapy, treatments for PTSD include prolonged exposure (Riggs, Cahill, and Foa 2007) and cognitive processing therapy (Shipherd, Street, and Resick 2006). They are interactive therapies that depend on actively targeting symptoms and helping the client reduce them to a point to which they interfere minimally in the person's daily life. Medications can be helpful for those who are highly anxious or those who are also suffering depression.

The most common effective treatment recommended for depression is cognitive behavioral therapy. This therapy focuses on increasing activity, particularly pleasant events, as a way to provide an initial improvement in mood. As the therapy progresses, the treatment focuses on helping the client to think more realistically and positively, as described in chapter 5 regarding hopeless thoughts and black-and-white thinking.

There are two widely used therapies for couples including integrative behavioral couple therapy (IBCT) (Jacobson and Christensen 1996) and emotion-focused couples therapy (Greenberg and Goldman 2008). Both are practiced in VA mental health services, and IBCT has recently been the focus of increased training throughout the Department of Veterans Affairs. These treatments for couples tend to focus on patterns of communication that become problematic and on understanding how to make adjustments that work better for the couple.

A range of other supportive talk therapies also can be helpful for veterans who need to work through questions of guilt, responsibility, and morality about their role in combat. These are highly important issues that can be overlooked when obvious symptoms of avoidance or low mood is the focus of treatment.

Online Resources

You will find a great deal of information available on websites associated with the US Department of Defense, the US Department of Veterans Affairs, nonprofit groups devoted to veterans' recovery and health, and on personal blogs. Below is a list of some of the most useful.

- A description of the range of services is available through the Department of Veterans Affairs mental health treatment services: http://www.mentalhealth.va.gov

- The website of a free telephone service for family members and friends concerned about a veteran, particularly about mental health issues, developed by the Department of Veterans Affairs: http://www.va.gov/coachingintocare

- Alcohol use guidelines from the US National Institutes of Health: http://www.niaaa.nih.gov/alcohol-health

- A comprehensive educational and outreach website focusing on post-traumatic stress disorder, developed by the Department of Veterans Affairs: http://www.ptsd.va.gov

- A free, online parenting program for military service members, veterans, and their spouses, developed by the Department of Defense and the Department of Veterans Affairs: http://www.militaryparenting.org and http://www.veteranparenting.org

- An online library of veterans' stories of their combat and recovery experiences, developed by the Department of Veterans Affairs: http://www.maketheconnection.net

- A free, online educational and life-coaching program that will help veterans to better handle life's challenges: http://www.startmovingforward.org

- An online resource supporting service members, their families, and veterans, with common postdeployment concerns, including post-traumatic stress disorder, traumatic brain injury, depression, anger, sleep problems, relationship concerns, and work adjustment, developed by the Department of Defense: http://www.AfterDeployment.org

- A reintegration and psychological health resource website developed by the Department of Defense for service members and their family members: http://www.RealWarriors.net

- An informational blog developed by the spouse of a combat veteran: http://patiencemason.blogspot.com

Final Words

Knowing when and how to seek mental health treatment can be a complicated journey, but fortunately there are many effective options available to you and your partner. The sign of the need for treatment is when your or your partner's feelings and behavior interfere with daily life. Typically this interference comes in the form of consistent distress and a decreased ability to be as effective and happy in work, relationships, and everyday tasks.

There are more treatment options available to you and your partner as a couple experiencing deployment and reintegration than at any previous time in US history. These options are available in government-sponsored efforts as well as in informal, volunteer, and nonprofit settings. It is still a difficult task, but it is important to note that there are many people who are interested in supporting you and your partner in your efforts to have a successful reintegration after deployment.

References

Accordino, M. P., and B. G. Guerney Jr. 2003. "Relationship Enhancement, Couples and Family Outcome Research of the Last Twenty Years." *Family Journal* 11(2): 162–66. doi: 10.1177/1066480702250146.

Adler, A. B., P. D. Bliese, D. McGurk, C. W. Hoge, and C. A. Castro. 2009. "Battlemind Debriefing and Battlemind Training as Early Interventions with Soldiers Returning from Iraq: Randomization by Platoon." *Journal of Consulting and Clinical Psychology* 77(5): 928–40. doi: 10.1037/a0016877.

Armstrong, K., S. Best, and P. Domenici. 2006. *Courage After Fire: Coping Strategies for Troops Returning from Iraq and Afghanistan and Their Families.* Berkeley, CA: Ulysses Press.

Batten, S. V., A. L. Drapalski, M. L. Decker, J. C. DeViva, L. J. Morris, M. A. Mann, and L. B. Dixon. 2009. "Veteran Interest in Family Involvement in PTSD Treatment." *Psychological Services* 6 (3): 184–89.

Belmont Jr., P. J., G. P. Goodman, B. Waterman, K. DeZee, R. Burks, and B. D. Owens. 2010. "Disease and Nonbattle Injuries Sustained by a US Army Brigade Combat Team During Operation Iraqi Freedom." *Military Medicine* 175(7): 469–76.

Carothers, B. J., and H. T. Reis. 2013. "Men and Women Are from Earth: Examining the Latent Structure of Gender." *Journal of Personality and Social Psychology* 104(2): 385–407. doi: 10.1037/a0030437.

Christensen, A., and N. S. Jacobson. 2000. *Reconcilable Differences.* New York: Guilford Press.

Epstein, N. 1985. "Depression and Marital Dysfunction: Cognitive and Behavioral Linkages." *International Journal of Mental Health* 13(3–4): 86–104.

Falloon, I. R. H., J. L. Boyd, and C. W. McGill. 1984. *Family Care of Schizophrenia: A Problem-Solving Approach to the Treatment of Mental Illness.* New York: Guilford Press.

Funk, J. L., and R. D. Rogge. 2007. "Testing the Ruler with Item Response Theory: Increasing Precision of Measurement for Relationship Satisfaction with the Couples Satisfaction Index." *Journal of Family Psychology* 21(4): 572–83.

Gottman, J. M. 2011. *The Science of Trust: Emotional Attunement for Couples.* New York: W. W. Norton and Company.

Gottman, J. M., and J. DeClaire. 2001. *The Relationship Cure: A Five-Step Guide to Strengthening Your Marriage, Family, and Friendships.* New York: Crown Publishing Group.

Greenberg, L. S., and R. N. Goldman. 2008. *Emotion-Focused Couples Therapy: The Dynamics of Emotion, Love, and Power.* Washington, DC: American Psychological Association.

Hoge, C. W., J. L. Auchterlonie, and C. S. Milliken. 2006. "Mental Health Problems, Use of Mental Health Services, and Attrition from Military Service after Returning from Deployment to Iraq or Afghanistan." *JAMA: Journal of the American Medical Association* 295(9): 1023–32. doi: 10.1001/jama.295.9.1023.

Jacobson, N. S., and A. Christensen. 1996. *Integrative Couple Therapy: Promoting Acceptance and Change.* New York: W. W. Norton and Company.

Karney, B. R., and J. S. Crown. 2007. *Families Under Stress: An Assessment of Data, Theory, and Research on Marriage and Divorce in the Military.* Arlington, VA: RAND Corporation.

MacDermid, S. M. 2006. "Multiple Transitions of Deployment and Reunion for Military Families." Presentation to the Office of Military Community and Family Policy (Office of the Secretary of Defense), Research Committee, Alexandria, VA, June 22, 2006.

McMahon, R. J., and J. S. Kotler. 2008. "Evidence-Based Therapies for Oppositional Behavior in Young Children." In *Handbook of Evidence-Based Therapies for Children and Adolescents,* edited by R. G. Steele,

T. D. Elkin, and M. C. Roberts, 221–40. New York: Springer Publishing.

Milliken, C. S., J. L. Auchterlonie, and C. W. Hoge. 2007. "Longitudinal Assessment of Mental Health Problems Among Active and Reserve Component Soldiers Returning from the Iraq War." *JAMA: Journal of the American Medical Association* 298(18): 2141–48.

Monson, C. M., S. J. Fredman, and K. C. Adair. 2008. "Cognitive-Behavioral Conjoint Therapy for Post-Traumatic Stress Disorder: Application to Operation Enduring and Iraqi Freedom Veterans." *Journal of Clinical Psychology* 64(8): 958–71. doi: 10.1002/jclp.20511.

Reis, H. T., M. Senchak, and B. Solomon. 1985. "Sex Differences in the Intimacy of Social Interaction: Further Examination of Potential Explanations." *Journal of Personality and Social Psychology* 48(5): 1204–17. doi: 10.1037/0022-3514.48.5.1204.

Reis, H. T., and P. Shaver. 1988. "Intimacy as an Interpersonal Process." In *Handbook of Personal Relationships: Theory, Research, and Interventions*, edited by S. Duck, 367–89. Oxford: John Wiley and Sons.

Renshaw, K. D., and S. B. Campbell. 2011. "Combat Veterans' Symptoms of PTSD and Partners' Distress: The Role of Partners' Perceptions of Veterans' Deployment Experiences." *Journal of Family Psychology* 25(6): 953–62. doi: 10.1037/a0025871.

Renshaw, K. D., C. S. Rodrigues, and D. H. Jones. 2008. "Psychological Symptoms and Marital Satisfaction in Spouses of Operation Iraqi Freedom Veterans: Relationship with Spouses' Perceptions of Veterans' Experiences and Symptoms." *Journal of Family Psychology* 22(4): 586–94. doi: 10.1037/0893-3200.22.3.586.

Rhoades, G. K., S. M. Stanley, and H. J. Markman. 2010. "Should I Stay or Should I Go? Predicting Dating Relationship Stability from Four Aspects of Commitment." *Journal of Family Psychology* 24(5): 543–50. doi: 10.1037/a0021008.

Riggs, D. S., S. P. Cahill, and E. B. Foa. 2007. "Prolonged Exposure Treatment of Post-Traumatic Stress Disorder." In *Cognitive-Behavioral Therapies for Trauma*, 2nd ed., edited by V. M. Follette and J. I. Ruzek, 65–95. New York: Guilford Press.

Ryan, R. M., and E. L. Deci. 2000. "Self-Determination Theory and the Facilitation of Intrinsic Motivation, Social Development, and Well-Being." *American Psychologist* 55(1): 68–78.

Sayers, S. L., V. A. Farrow, J. Ross, and D. W. Oslin. 2009. "Family Problems Among Recently Returned Military Veterans Referred for a Mental Health Evaluation." *Journal of Clinical Psychiatry* 70(2): 163–70. doi: 10.4088/JCP.07m03863.

Sayers, S. L., and R. E. Heyman. 2002. "Behavioral Couples Therapy." In *Textbook of Family and Couples Therapy: Clinical Applications*, edited by G. P. Sholevar and L. D. Schwoeri, 461–500. Arlington, VA: American Psychiatric Publishing.

Shipherd, J. C., A. E. Street, and P. A. Resick. 2006. "Cognitive Therapy for Post-Traumatic Stress Disorder." In *Cognitive-Behavioral Therapies for Trauma*, 2nd ed., edited by V. M. Follette and J. I. Ruzek, 96–116. New York: Guilford Press.

Wilson, S. R. 2002. *Seeking and Resisting Compliance: Why People Say What They Do When Trying to Influence Others.* Thousand Oaks, CA: Sage Publications.

Steven L. Sayers, PhD, is associate professor of psychology in the department of psychiatry at the Perelman School of Medicine at the University of Pennsylvania. He is director of the Advanced Fellowship Program in Mental Illness Research and Treatment at the Philadelphia Veterans Affairs Medical Center. Sayers has published numerous articles regarding the role of family members and other social supports in mental and physical health.

Foreword writer **Keith Armstrong, LCSW**, is clinical professor of psychiatry at the University of California, San Francisco. He is director of the San Francisco Veterans Administration's (SFVA) Family Therapy Program and the City College of San Francisco Veterans Outreach Program, and is a member of the SFVA's PTSD Clinical Team. In addition, he is a consultant for the Intensive Family Therapy program at the University of California, San Francisco. Armstrong has authored numerous clinical and research articles and chapters addressing the treatment of traumatized individuals and families. He is also a reviewer for the *Journal of Traumatic Stress*, a top journal in the field of traumatology, and he has conducted numerous radio, newspaper, and podcast interviews on the psychological treatment of veterans and families. He lives with his wife and two children in the San Francisco Bay Area.

FROM OUR PUBLISHER—

As the publisher at New Harbinger and a clinical psychologist since 1978, I know that emotional problems are best helped with evidence-based therapies. These are the treatments derived from scientific research (randomized controlled trials) that show what works. Whether these treatments are delivered by trained clinicians or found in a self-help book, they are designed to provide you with proven strategies to overcome your problem.

Therapies that aren't evidence-based—whether offered by clinicians or in books—are much less likely to help. In fact, therapies that aren't guided by science may not help you at all. That's why this New Harbinger book is based on scientific evidence that the treatment can relieve emotional pain.

This is important: if this book isn't enough, and you need the help of a skilled therapist, use the following resource to find a clinician trained in the evidence-based protocols appropriate for your problem.

Real help is available for the problems you have been struggling with. The skills you can learn from evidence-based therapies will change your life.

Matthew McKay, PhD
Publisher, New Harbinger Publications

**If you need a therapist, the following organization
can help you find a therapist trained in cognitive behavioral therapy (CBT).**

The Association for Behavioral & Cognitive Therapies (ABCT) Find-a-Therapist service offers a list of therapists schooled in CBT techniques. Therapists listed are licensed professionals who have met the membership requirements of ABCT and who have chosen to appear in the directory.

Please visit www.abct.org and click on *Find a Therapist*.

**For additional support for patients, family, and friends,
please contact the following:**

National Center for PTSD
visit www.ptsd.va.gov

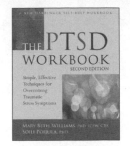

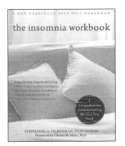
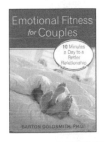